Cheryl has written this life-changi with you in mind. You will find encouragement! You will be inspired! Because of that, I highly recommend this book. Get your copy! Your life will never be the same.

—Apostle Dr. Dezrene Robinson

My wife Cheryl has lived an exemplary life. She has shown how you can bounce back, no matter what life may throw at you. She encourages me to believe I can accomplish anything. According to Philippians 4:13, *"I can do all things through him who strengthens me"* (ESV). I know this book will help you to look at life differently—to not see yourself as a victim, but as a victor.

—Pastor Wade N. Edwards

Cheryl and I go way back. She has been a true friend and an encourager. Cheryl has overcome so many obstacles and I am happy that she has decided to tell her story. Her story is very powerful and captivating. After reading *A Brand New Horizon*, you will realize that you are never without hope, no matter how low life gets. Furthermore, you will overcome every obstacle life throws at you and be convinced that God is not done with you.

—Shafay R. Hutchinson

Cheryl B. Edwards is a woman with a message. In this beautifully written biography, she takes the reader on her own personal journey of triumph over defeat. If you want to be encouraged and inspired, look no further. *A Brand New Horizon* is much more than a biography or a good read, it has been a labour of love and is testimony to the truth that no destructive force in our lives is greater than God's plan to redeem it all.

—Reverend Gillian Anderson

In this book by Cheryl B. Edwards, she writes about running the race, making discoveries, and experiencing redeeming love. However, she also shares with great authenticity about deep loneliness, struggling for acceptance, taking a dark detour, and derailed dreams. She vividly expresses her frustrated efforts to validate the identity she desired for herself through her career as a celebrated athlete.

Cheryl celebrates the transformation of the Lord's redeeming love, which found her despite rejection and deep-rooted feelings of condemnation. Readers will benefit much from Cheryl's openness about her own mental health diagnosis, which wonderfully does not become a part of her identity.

Hope eventually dawns for Cheryl, accompanied by a song of victory. Keep watch for more words and more songs to definitely arise from this "brand-new horizon."

—Rev. Peggy I. Kennedy, Two Silver Trumpets Ministries
Author of *A Is for Apple*, *Hear the Sound*, and *Chosen*

Cheryl B. Edwards invites readers into her private life and the challenges she faced while growing up. She puts herself in a vulnerable position by addressing the elephant in the room while giving hope to others in similar situations. This book is a must read for anyone who has ever wondered about the endless possibilities that God opens up to those who allow him to bring a message out of their mess.

—Lilian Kelani, BScN,

Host of The Shyft wellness Center and Social Entrepreneur

God has blessed my daughter Cheryl with a unique intellect, as well as a heart of love and integrity to minister to hurting women and youth nationwide. God is doing a new thing in and through her.

Writing this book has taken her to a higher level in her Christian walk and close fellowship with the Lord. I do believe that she has been chosen to bring the message across that God is able to heal us everywhere it hurts—be it physical, emotional, or spiritual—and that He makes the dark clouds dissipate. As you look towards the eastern skies, the sun will shine again on this brand-new horizon.

—Eda Allen, Cheryl's mom

Cheryl writes, "Challenges in life are always good. When we're challenged to step out of our comfort zones, we put aside the familiar and embark on change!" I believe that this book might make some a little uncomfortable, and at times even a little afraid, but what I do know is this: it will force your faith to rise and encourage you to let your roots grow deeper and change some misguided beliefs about yourself and even God. Are you willing to be uncomfortable?

God has indeed got Cheryl on a journey to a brand-new horizon, with many challenges and seasons of growth, and I am blessed to have a front row seat. It's remarkable to see how Cheryl is learning to cling to her heavenly Father the way she clung to her earthly father. And now you get to experience it too.

Are struggling to be free, or needing protection from the dark places that frighten you or threaten to hold you back? Maybe you just need your faith to be renewed. I believe that as you read this book, you will see how with God all things are possible, if you only believe. Believe in your brand-new horizon.

—Rev. Vahen King

Author, international speaker, and founder of Going Farther

Cheryl's story is both heartbreaking and inspirational. Our friendship takes us from our teen years to the present. I've seen her go through the depths of depression to the joys of marriage, from experiencing loss, in more ways than one, to seeing God granting her victory on the mountain top!

This book will take you on an experiential journey of many emotions. But through it all, Cheryl had God on her side. She also has her parents, who prayed fervently; close friends, who were with her through it all; and a husband who loves her in spite of it all. Prepare yourself for the shifting of a woman's mind and heart as she faces many giants to the mighty move of God that turned mourning into rejoicing and gave her beauty for ashes.

—Stacey Tyndale-Brown

A BRAND New

HORIZON

An Autobiography

CHERYL B. EDWARDS

A BRAND NEW HORIZON
Copyright © 2021 by Cheryl B. Edwards

Printed in Canada

ISBN: 978-1-4866-2143-9
eBook ISBN: 978-1-4866-2144-6

Word Alive Press
119 De Baets Street Winnipeg, MB R2J 3R9
www.wordalivepress.ca

Cataloguing in Publication information can be obtained from Library and Archives Canada.

This book is dedicated to the memory of my late father,

Harvey C. Allen,

a man who believed that I could fly without wings.

CONTENTS

ACKNOWLEDGEMENTS

An old friend of mine would pose this question: when are you going to write your book? You need to write your story!

Even back then, I felt the pressure was on.

Little did I know that God was preparing me to write my story in and through my life experiences. I spent so much time writing in my journal, starting and then stopping, and repeat. I never dreamt it would be even remotely possible to write a full autobiography.

When I spoke with Jen from Word Alive Press, she asked me to forward her my outline and share my testimony. After I shared my story, she encouraged me to write the book, assuring me that I had a huge testimony to share with the world.

Upon hearing that it was possible to write my story, I was reminded what God had said to me in my younger years. Is there anything too hard for God?

I give honour first and foremost to my personal Lord and Saviour Jesus Christ, for without Him I am nothing. Wherever I go, the Lord is with me. He gave me the strength to carry on and to finish this autobiography in style! For that, I will never stop praising and thanking Him for His grace in fulfilling my dream.

Well over a decade, I met Reverend Peggy Kennedy. I will never forget the prophetic word she imparted to me. She prophesied that I was running from well to well, and that Jesus wanted me to drink from *the* well from which I would never thirst again. It has been such an honour to reconnect with her again. Thank you for allowing God to use you to pour His goodness into my heart. Bless you.

My mom has always been one of my greatest cheerleaders. She always said, "Cheryl, you have it in you and you can do it!" Even through writing this book during my darkest times, Mom cheered me on. Although my dad isn't here today, Mom is my friend and greatest motivator. She believed in me even when I couldn't believe in myself.

When I was going through a tough time and searching for answers, God led me to a woman of God who simply said, "Read the word." That person is Pastor Ingrid Belle. One thing I learned through this experience was to get to know God for yourself. There were times when I was running from church to church, running on empty—and now God is grounding me in Him and anchoring me in His truth. Thank you, Pastor Ingrid, for believing in me and pouring out the wisdom I hold to dearly this very day.

A year ago, I met Apostle Dr. Dezerene Robinson. She saw the calling of my life and challenged me to *push* through the rocky roads, to *push* even when I felt broken, despondent, and despaired. She let me know that I was passing through the refiner's fire, assuring me that when I came out, I would come out as pure gold. Apostle Dr. Dezerene was another cheerleader who loved me for who I was and accepted me during my ups and downs. Thank you, Apostle Dezerene, for helping me to *push*.

To my editor, Evan, thank you for always encouraging me to press on, chapter after chapter. Thank you for your honesty and simplicity in the development of my autobiography.

To my dearest sister in Christ and friend, Vahen King, thank you for being my prayer partner and friend. You are a solid friend who also helped get me to the next level of *push*. She was like a midwife interceding and praying in the birthing room. Thank you, Vahen, for your honesty and transparency and encouraging me to go higher.

I also have to mention my long-time friend Shafay Hutchinson. Through the thick and thin, you were there to pray with me, encourage me, and uplift my soul. No matter how big my dreams were, you always encouraged me to dream big. Thank you, Shafay, for being a part of this journey with me and God bless you for being who you are! You are more than a conqueror through Christ Jesus. I love you much, my friend.

And I will never forget when I met my Boaz, Wade Nicolas Edwards, who is my solid rock and sounding board. My husband played a huge role in developing this book. He was an editor affording me sound advice. To my husband, lover, and friend, thank you for being who you are, a man of integrity. Bless you richly for taking the time to encourage me and motivating me to keep pressing forward, even in times when I wanted to give up. For that reason, I love you even more than I ever have before. Thank you.

INTRODUCTION

Imagine a little girl trapped, consumed by fear, and bound by invisible chains that prohibit her voice from being heard. Struggling to fit in and feel accepted, she faces one rejection after another.

How tragic! This little girl is trying to fit in and be included, yet she is teased and continues to struggle with her identity, always trying to emulate someone she is not. The loud noise of rejection echoes in her young mind, eventually producing such deep-seated pain that it manifests in demonic warfare that nearly costs the girl her very life!

This little girl is me.

Fearfully and wonderfully made—that's how God created me. And from a young age, I knew this to be true. I had an earthly farther who told me I was loved and believed I could fly without wings. He modelled the love of my heavenly Father.

However, that reality eventually faded as I walked through failed dreams, a loss of identity, demoniac oppression, and utter despair. Soon I was running in fear and wondering why I had been made.

When I was in a dark place, I wrote the following lyrics:

Have you ever felt alone?
When you are in the valley and you feel all hope is gone?
Just call on Jesus and He will comfort you.
Oh, let Your Spirit come into my soul!

When I wrote this, I was haunted by fond memories of joy and happiness. I wanted desperately to feel loved and free again, but all I could see were shadows. The agony of my hopelessness and despair saturated my soul with fear.

This dark place is called Lo-debar, a place of no communication located in the middle of nowhere. It was the name of a town in biblical times where Mephibosheth, the grandson of King Saul, lived as a young child. When his father and grandfather were killed in an attack, Mephibosheth's nurse fled, and in the process he was dropped. As a result, he became crippled in both feet and couldn't walk.

Can anyone relate to a place like this, where it feels like all hope is lost, like the loneliness is embedded so deep in your soul that no one can reach or touch you? Have you ever felt rejected from all sides? Have insecurities been your closest friend? Have you ever felt insignificant, worthless, and hopeless?

I can honestly say that I experienced firsthand the powers of darkness. They assaulted my physical, mental, and spiritual well-being.

The enemy's strategic plan is to kill and rob us of everything.

The thief does not come except to steal, and to kill, and to destroy. I have come that they may have life, and that they may have it more abundantly. (John 10:10, NKJV)

Satan is after our minds to torment and feed us lies.

When he speaks a lie, he speaks from his own resources, for he is a liar and the father of it. (John 8:44, NKJV)

When the enemy comes to feed our minds with lies, we must replace it with God's Word. Once you replace the lie with the truth, you become free to unlock the chains to the prison doors that hold you captive.

And you shall know the truth, and the truth shall make you free. (John 8:32, NKJV)

The enemy will even attempt to entice us with things that could lead us into addiction, abuse, and gang warfare. He is a thief and we must not succumb to his evil schemes.

...lest Satan should take advantage of us; for we are not ignorant of his devices. (2 Corinthians 2:11, NKJV)

One thing I know is that the enemy used my mind like a playground, tormenting me with voices, thoughts of suicide, self-sabotage, and condemnation. This reminds me of one of my favourite scriptures:

There is therefore now no condemnation to those who are in Christ Jesus, who do not walk according to the flesh, but according to the Spirit. (Romans 8:1, NKJV)

The enemy can tell us lies and fill our minds with deceit, causing us to spiral into deep depression, fear, and even oppression.

Mental illness is defined as a condition that affects a person's thoughts, emotions, or mood. Such a condition may affect someone's ability to relate to others and function each day. Mental health, however, refers to a person's condition regarding their psychological and emotional wellbeing. This includes the ability to learn, feel, express, and manage a range of positive and negative emotions. It also includes the ability to form and maintain good relationships with others.

In my case, doctors had no clue what to diagnose me with. They tried to label me with many things, but the labels didn't stick.

One thing I know is that no matter the trial, God has a greater plan for you. The Bible says that *"He who is in you is greater than he who is in the world"* (1 John 4:4, NKJV).

I understand all too well how the devil can oppress and rob us of our joy and livelihood. But I also understand how God can come into our lives and make all things new. The Bible reminds us, *"Therefore if anyone is in Christ, he is a new creation; old things have passed away; behold, all things have become new"* (2 Corinthians 5:17, NKJV).

If Jesus Christ can take a lump of clay and turn it into something beautiful, we must take courage. He is a gracious Father who has compassion on His children. We are His treasure and we are fearfully and wonderfully made in His sight.

Although it was challenging to cope, I had to remind myself of God's promises towards me.

One of the promises God assured me of comes from Jeremiah 29:11: *"For I know the thoughts that I think toward you, says the Lord, thoughts of peace and not of evil, to give you a future and a hope"* (NKJV). In other words, no matter how hopeless you may feel, and no matter your present situation, God has a plan for your life.

As a former track and field athlete who competed for Canada for years, I know what it feels like to fall into a dark pit. But then I received redemption through Christ!

My desire is to impact, inspire, and encourage you. My prayer is that through reading my story, you will come to know that nothing is impossible with God. If you've never experienced genuine love from a father, know that there is a loving Father who loves you with an everlasting love (Jeremiah 31:3).

Finally, God desires for you to know who you are in Him. What does God say about you? Take the time to know Him and discover freedom through developing a relationship with Him and understanding the Word of God.

Once you've read this book, you will understand my journey and witness how such a loving Father redeemed His daughter from death and destruction, giving me victory and redemption! You'll also find some nuggets to help you to identify your truest potential.

Come with me on a journey as we proceed towards a brand-new horizon and discover how God turned my test into a testimony.

Chapter One

I REMEMBER WHEN

I remember when my dad and I would go walking in the park. I can still smell the fresh pine trees and acorns. I can see the pitter-patter of little squirrels around Victoria Park. I remember my little feet kicking the ball, and then anticipating that Dad would kick it back to me.

Oh, how I loved my father. A man who was a friend of God, a man who believed in me even when I couldn't believe in myself. A man who shared poetic metaphors, like a caterpillar emerging into a beautiful butterfly or watching a spider build its web. He shared about true friends—and if you had two, you were fortunate. My father was my biggest supporter, and can you tell? I was a daddy's girl.

I remember the starter commanding us athletes to get on our marks in the Butterdome at the Edmonton Journal Games. It was the two-hundred-metre dash and my dad sat in the stands. Our eyes locked and we both nodded in agreement. I lowered myself into the starting blocks.

"On your mark! Set!"

The gun went off!

The race was clocked and finished in a matter of seconds. I won that race!

My Grade Six teacher formed a game called Percyball, a game similar to tackle ball, pitting the girls against the boys. When I caught the ball, I ran for my life and the girls won!

My elementary school coach had me join the jogging club, and my first competition was the C.A.P.E.R. run. While running through the forest, I gasped for air and wondered why I was doing this. I kept daydreaming, until before I knew it I realized I had crossed the finish line and won my very first cross-country run. The medal ceremony was presented by a former Canadian Olympian.

Track and field played a huge role in my life. While trying to keep up with my academics, I always preferred to prepare for the next championship. I remained committed to this sport for seventeen years, having started at the tender age of nine and finally retiring at twenty-six.

Back in the Day

My very first birthday was a day full of balloons, cake, and friends. Meanwhile, Mom and her friend were trying their best to fit the perfect skinny dress on a chubby baby! Can you imagine? They had to cut the sleeves to make my arms fit!

Well, it's a good thing I didn't understand the meaning of embarrassment.

To make matters worse, my childhood friend decided that, just maybe, he could have the privilege of blowing out my first candle! I was not happy with that! I had to figure out, is this my birthday or is it his?

All the same, birthdays were always a blessing and something to look forward to. Mom ensured that we always had chocolate cake with one extra candle each year.

Growing up in Edmonton, I had the privilege of having some cherished childhood friends. One of these friends and I would sing songs from the early 80s, maybe with the hope of someone discovering our talent! Although we were closet singers.

But soon my friend passed, dying of a brain aneurism, and I was so heartbroken. This was the first person I was close with who passed away. When a dear friend passes on, you only realize how much you miss them after they're gone and the pain lingers. But eventually you realize that life goes on, and so I had to move on.

Some of my fondest childhood memories involve being able to travel to sunny Jamaica, attend family gatherings, and on special occasions go to amazing restaurants to dine, laugh, and understand the true meaning of family.

My mom recently reminded me of the time when my parents and friends took me on a trip to Banff, Alberta. I was three. They decided to have lunch and seated me in a highchair — but I had grown tired of highchairs and had decided it was time to sit in a regular chair. I cried to bits and everyone started panicking. But after they placed me in a regular chair, the crying stopped.

Sometimes in life we get so comfortable with the familiar, whether it's with relationships, schools, or even jobs. But then there are times when God wants to elevate us to another level, to dream and reach our highest potential.

You see, even at three years of age, the highchair had become too familiar for me. Now it was time to step out from the familiar and soar a little higher—into the unfamiliar.

Challenges in life are always good. When we're challenged to step out of our comfort zones, we put aside the familiar and embark on change!

A Girl's Best Friend

My mom is such a gift to this world. When I think of her, I think of the song by Bette Middler, "Wind Beneath My Wings." My mom is truly the wind beneath my wings. She's a virtuous woman of God. According to Proverbs 3:15, *"She is more precious than rubies, and all the things you may desire cannot compare with her"* (NKJV).

Mom is the eldest of eight siblings and she grew up with her grandmother, Bernice Grant, who would be my great-grandmother. My middle name is Bernice, and I am so honoured to have been named after her.

When my mom was two years of age, she lost her father and thereafter didn't have the opportunity to experience having a father in the home. However, I come from a lineage of strong women of faith who were virtuous and exemplified strength, courage, and dignity for their family, friends, and community. Mom was my tower of strength growing up, especially during times of rebellion when my mouth was extremely feisty, without apology!

All the same, Mom was able to give to her only child that which she'd never had: the opportunity to celebrate birthdays, graduations, and of course attend events like track meets. She was always the loudest in the stands! Everyone in the crowd would know that was my mom cheering for me.

Mom also took me to see many movies. She enrolled me in ballet, jazz, and piano. But I have to say I was very uncoordinated when it came to dance. It's one thing to dance on your own, and a whole other thing to dance along with others! That's a challenge.

And when it came to singing, my voice was always the loudest— to the point that my dad had to tell me to stop yelling. But no matter where I was singing, my mom figured I was always the best one there.

But she wasn't particularly keen on me eating at other people's houses. One of my fondest childhood memories involved me defying that rule and going to my childhood friend's house for supper on my own terms—only to meet Mom at the front door with her famous brown slipper to give me the whooping of my life! Each time she spanked me, she was reminding me to never do this again. Me and that slipper weren't friends. Of course I eventually learned not to make history repeat itself.

My mom taught me so much, including to believe in myself and appreciate how God made me. She truly is my sounding board and a girl's best friend, and I will be forever grateful for all the sacrifices she has made for me.

Matters of the Heart

At a very tender age, I went through a season of sexual abuse that caused me to have insecurity, low self-esteem, fear, rejection, and identity issues. The way I dealt with my insecurities and emotions was to suffer silently.

Through that silence, it became particularly challenging to maintain relationships, because although I was very loving, I often didn't know how to trust or keep a friend for a long period of time. Growing into my adolescent years, I wore layers of masks, making it hard to identify who I really was. I was always trying to be someone I was not.

In the world today, we see a lot of picture-perfect women with long hair and impeccable features. I was never satisfied with how God made me. I wanted to change my hair every week and was always fascinated by the latest hairdos, even if the style wasn't suitable for me.

My dad owned one of the top beauty salons in Edmonton and my dear aunt, who managed the salon, always went into hiding when I came around. I would demand to get my hair done—on a weekly basis, or maybe every other week. And who knows? My aunt may still be in hiding, but thank God I left vanity at the back door.

If you think that was bad, I once flew all the way to New York just to get my hair done.

From Jheri curls to braids to weaves to wigs... you name it, I've done it all! I very well could write a memoir on what not to do with your hair! With the amount of money I spent on my hair, I could have owned my own home, paid in full.

I always wanted my features to mirror what I saw in magazines. I wore so much makeup that people could hardly recognize me. I genuinely had to come to a place of accepting myself, learning to love myself for who I was and appreciating how God made me.

I'm reminded of what Scripture says about us being *"fearfully and wonderfully made"* (Psalm 139:14, NKJV). And in Ecclesiastes 3:11, God calls us beautiful. I had to take a good look at myself in the mirror and remind myself how beautiful God had made me.

I finally came to the realization that we are all unique and we need to know how special we are. We are royalty, handpicked from our Creator to make a difference in this universe.

My insecurities ran deep. I was one of those children who was always the outcast. No matter how hard I tried, I was never able to fit in. In the comforts of my home, I was in my safe place, especially in my room where the radio echoed classical music. The soothing music took my imagination to faraway lands, permitting me to escape the realities of insecurity and fear.

As a young child, fear was my worst enemy. I was always afraid to speak and use my voice to be heard. Doubts and thoughts of inadequacy invaded my mind.

One thing I'd like to make clear is this: the enemy will attempt to pull us away from where God is trying to take us, and children can be the most vulnerable when they listen to the teasing and negative thoughts provoked by their peers. It's important that parents teach their children that words have power. If these words aren't dealt with immediately, they can take up residence in our minds and create strongholds.

In one way or another, someone might have attacked you through words that pierced your very soul, and you never were able to shake it off. I refer to this as mind wars, and it's something I'll expound upon in later chapters.

It took me two decades to come to the realization that it's okay to love me. That it's okay to forgive myself and to love others, even those who turned against me. The Bible says that we must even love our enemies and pray for those who curse and persecute us (Matthew 5:44). God will avenge those who have wronged us (Luke 18:7), and He will fight our battles for us. All we need to do is be still and know that He is God (Psalm 46:10). This also reminds me of the time when Moses told the Israelites that they only needed to be still and watch for the salvation of the Lord (Exodus 14:4).

It's okay if I don't have long hair that goes down my back, or features that resemble a celebrity. When I look in the mirror, bare-faced, I can now appreciate how the Potter made me. I had to go down to the Potter's house several times for healing and deliverance, and there I found peace and joy—the joy of knowing who God is, and that I could come to Him at any given moment. The Lord had to perform a spiritual surgery in me and make me over again.

Whether I'm broken or torn, I know it gives God great joy to take me just as I am and mend my broken and wounded soul. That is the amazing thing about the God I serve: He is a God of second chances.

My Reflection

When my dad gave his life to the Lord Jesus, he never looked back. His testament was by divine appointment.

For a while my parents lived in Owensboro, Kentucky while my dad did contract work. They attended a local church for the duration of their stay, and one Sunday the church had a special service during which all the pews were full.

During the sermon, the senior pastor paused and his eyes turned directly to my dad.

"Sir!" the preacher said. "Jesus is calling you!"

Who, me? he thought, pointing back at himself in astonishment.

Finally he went up to the altar and the pastor led him through the sinner's prayer. Soon after, Dad wanted to go all the way; he added his name to the list of people to get baptized.

His life was never the same after that. The things of his past were in the past and he was a brand-new creation in Christ. Having had a former addiction to alcohol, God gave him a new thirst to drink from the well which would never leave him thirsty again.

My father was one of my biggest supporters in whatever I put my mind to do. He believed that if my profession were law, I would be an excellent lawyer. After all, I had the gift of gab!

Although school was always a challenge for me, he always believed I was the smartest child he had ever known, which allowed me to believe in myself and have full confidence that anything is possible.

I relished in reasoning with my dad, as we were both visionaries. No matter how big the vision, he enhanced it by supporting my dream. Still, I always wondered at the back of my mind: could these dreams really be actualized?

Although I was a believer in Christ, my dad had a type of faith only God could give him—and I always desired to have that same type of faith. Even when you couldn't see it, he would speak it into being, and it would come to pass. He had what I would call Abrahamic faith!

Music runs on both sides of my family. Sometimes people would ask me where I got my ability to sing, and to be quite honest, it's from the Lord. The Lord gave me this gift, and I choose to nurture it and use it for His glory.

I mentioned earlier that I struggled with insecurity and fear for years. My dad had the same struggle, and as I became more mature in Christ I realized that this was a generational curse. My dad would be fearful to speak to a crowd of people, while I too would be petrified to deliver a message or sing. Everything I did was magnified by fear!

Over the years, as my dad grew strong in his faith, I noticed that his fear dissipated. Once he confronted it, he believed that nothing was impossible with God. He believed with all his heart that God hadn't given him *"a spirit of fear, but of power and of love and of a sound mind"* (2 Timothy 1:7, NKJV).

The last time I spent with my dad, we ate pizza in the park. I just listened to his sound wisdom and encouragement to pursue my dreams.

Unfortunately, he didn't have the opportunity to live and see my dreams unfold. On November 6, 2013, my dad passed away. His final words were, "Lord, I am ready to come home to be with you. Please do not have me here to suffer. I do not want anyone to attend to my private needs."

Dad was loved and supported by his family, church family, and friends. He had mentored young men, given to those less fortunate, and even prayed for others to receive Christ as their personal Lord and Saviour.

I am reminded of this scripture: *"And the King will answer and say to them, 'Assuredly, I say to you, inasmuch as you did it to one of the least of these My brethren, you did it to Me'"* (Matthew 25:40, NKJV).

I miss my dad, and I often wish he were here just to talk, to be a sounding board. But one thing I know is that my dad loved me, and his legacy lives on. He meant the world to me, and when he died it felt as if a piece of me also died.

However, I would soon learn that there is a greater love, one found only in Jesus, for He is the father of the fatherless.

Chapter Two

STAY IN YOUR LANE

I once heard a preacher say, "God is like Coke! He's the real thing." In that moment, this man of God allowed my little mind to believe that God is real. For those who may have doubted God is real, he reminded us through his preaching with power, authority, and conviction that there is a God.

I grew up in the church, attending Calvary Temple at an early age. A young sister in Christ picked me up every Sunday.

Every now and then, I recollect the preacher of that church, so radical and passionate for Christ. My eyes would remain steady on him, witnessing the Holy Spirit moving!

From as early as I can remember, I've had a love for God I cannot explain. As 1 John 4:19 tells us, *"We love God because he first loved us"* (ESV).

An only child is a lonely child. Even when I was in a crowd, I still felt lonely. When Sunday morning came, I would find solace at church and have comradery with the other youth I met there.

In later years I attended Shiloh Baptist Church, where my aunt took me to church every Sunday. I sat beside her every week without fail. She always had gum in her purse. Anyone who knew me knew that when church felt like it would never end, my mind would wander to food and I'd ask myself what we were going to have for supper. My aunt would offer me a small piece of gum, not enough to satisfy me—and it certainly couldn't replace spaghetti and meatballs, one of the dishes, by the way, my mom so skillfully made. I'd swallow up the gum, and meanwhile I'd still be hungry, anticipating the end of the service so I could satisfy my appetite.

A love of music was instilled in me from such an early age. Both my mother and father owned a wide selection of music that filled our home.

While I had been attending Calvary Temple, I was once part of a children's singalong. It aired on television, so when it was my turn to sing I felt so nervous that I thought my heart would beat right out of my chest. That was the first time I got some exposure from singing, and I soon developed a passion for music. While I attended Edmonton Community Worship Hour Church, our choir was extremely joyful and charismatic in our praise.

I grew up in the church choir, meaning that I grew up on gospel music. I absolutely loved that type of music, and I still do to this very day. Whenever I felt despair or lonely, gospel music would soothe my soul.

But I was never comfortable or satisfied with my voice. I figured that if my voice was even one-quarter as good as Whitney Houston's, I would be good.

I'll never forget the time when the church's senior pastor asked me to come and sing a solo piece at church one morning. After I finished the solo, my pastor teared up and said, "This girl can sing."

I'll always remember those who have impacted my life in one way or another. That pastor was not only a respected leader of our church, he was also my mentor and spiritual father.

The church was multicultural. After all, when we get to heaven we'll see people of all nationalities, colours, and creeds. I believe the colour of our skin should never be a concern, though it separates us; through Christ and the cross, Jesus conjoins us as one race—and that is the human race.

Teenage Days

Although I was an avid churchgoer, I had my share of teenage rebellion. At one point in my twenties, I thought my mom wanted to make a run from it—"it" being all my waywardness and backwardness. But instead she loved me throughout the process of my adolescence.

At fourteen, I was adamant about going to a nightclub with my aunt and uncle, provided that my parents gave me the green light. When I posed the question to my mom, it didn't cross her mind to think about it. She flat-out refused. My reaction was a mixture of pity party and rage. I was extremely devastated that this precocious teenager wouldn't be able to attend a nightclub that was only suitable for those eighteen years and older. Imagine that?

When I was at an age to go nightclubs, I danced every Saturday night and then caught up with my worship and praise on Sunday morning. Every week I found myself at the nightclubs, and just a sip of wine alone was enough to make me delusional and send me spinning. I guess me and alcohol don't mix. I was never a smoker or a drinker, just a young girl who wanted to fit in wherever she could.

Bright and early on Sunday mornings, my pastor would know what I had been up to, based on how sober me and my friends looked. He would call us out to sing, regardless of how we felt. And even if we grumbled or snickered under our breath, obedience was the order of the day.

All in all, church was my place of refuge and my pastor demonstrated love, patience, and impartiality. He truly exemplified the fruit of the spirit (Galatians 5:22–23) and my brothers and sisters in Christ showed love and support.

The mothers and grandmothers of the church always reminded me to wear my stockings and dress warm. And of course, I respected my elders—although wearing stockings at an early age wasn't particularly my thing, and still isn't.

Most of all, despite my mess, God loved me. He always showed grace towards me, and his lovingkindness is from everlasting to everlasting. I just love the Lord.

As I look back over my life, I see myself as the prodigal daughter. I strayed, wandering off to do things my own way. Meanwhile, God's hand was always my compass, bringing me back home and giving me a second chance.

Run for It

Ever since I can remember, I've enjoyed running. Whether in a park, an open field, or through an alley, I would be running. The joy of being a child is that you get to discover the talents that come naturally to you—and for me, it was running.

I started going to jogging club in elementary school, and from the moment I won my first race I realized I wanted to pursue this. School was always a challenge for me, but track and field opened many doors. The sport catapulted me from everyday life into local, national, and even international competitions and recognitions.

My success in track-and-field was quite extensive. At the Women's Colgate Games, I was awarded athlete of the year in the fourteen- to fifteen-year-olds division for the hundred-metre dash. I was a three-time national junior champion and also competed at the World Junior Championships in Athens, Greece and Sudbury, Ontario.

I then attended the World Championships in Tokyo, Japan, earning sixth place in the women's four-by-four relay, breaking the Canadian record. I was the two-time Pan Am junior champion in both Sante Fe, Argentina and Kingston, Jamaica in the women's four-hundred-metre dash.

Later, I was a bronze medallist in the women's four-by-four relay at the Commonwealth Games in Auckland, New Zealand. In the women's three-hundred-metre dash, I earned the record at the Cargill Games. Thereafter I held several provincial records. And finally, in 1990, I received the Harry Jerome Awards in Toronto, Ontario.

Track and field was my hideaway, a place where I could escape from the noise of the world. Whenever I desired to get away, I made an escape to the field grounds and walked around, reflecting on and attempting to reason out the fragments of my life. I harboured a lot of pain and rejection and was always concerned about what others said about me or the way they perceived me. If I saw my peers talking about me, or even whispering my name, I immediately cringed. Anxiety would set in, causing me to become a recluse, not allowing anyone inside the giant wall I'd built.

Running was a natural gift for me, but I had so much going on in terms of the battlefield of the mind. I longed to feel accepted but still felt alone. I would work myself to a frenzy trying to be a people-pleaser, all the while striving to maintain my championship titles in the junior division. I had absolutely no balance in my life, just a lot of instability.

I was very much driven by competition and strove to maintain perfection. But as my journey progressed, I had to come to the harsh reality that no one is perfect, only God. As Psalm 18:30 says, *"This God—his way is perfect; the word of the Lord proves true; he is a shield for all those who take refuge in him"* (ESV).

Like any sport, track and field has its trials and triumphs, and even some windy roads. I met some wonderful friends along my running journey. Some have gone their separate ways, while others I still hold very dear to my heart.

One childhood friend of mine always made me laugh while we attended practices. She was prone to early injuries, and no matter how often she explained to our coach that she was in pain, he always had a hard time believing the story.

And let us not forget that in the track club, I trained with men. There were few women present. Training with the guys was always a challenge. Because they were stronger, faster, and it was always hard to compete with them.

All the athletes I trained with were amazingly talented. However, my coach and I bickered frequently, often because I was trying to opt out of training. Sometimes I was so lazy to train that I would rather go to the mall and delve into fresh cinnamon buns. In fact, after I worked out I would hit the mall and feast on junk food! There's really something wrong with that picture.

Overall, I was determined to be a world champion. Although that dream was never actualized, God had a different plan. I would plan, and plan some more, but I have to be reminded that as we plan, our steps are ordered by the Lord (Psalm 37:23).

When it comes to personal achievements, especially sports, you only get what you put in. We all have gifts, but I had to learn the hard way that I had to put into practice the gifts God had blessed me with. It was essential that I acquire enough discipline so I could share these gifts with the world for the glory of God. We must never take our gifts for granted, and most of all never take for granted the one who is the giver of good gifts.

Finish Well

In life, my parents taught me the four Ds: dedication, desire, discipline, and determination. Dedication is to be committed to the task at hand, desire is to obtain hope concerning your goals, discipline is to exhibit self-control, and determination is to finish well. I learned all these attributes as an athlete, and I still exemplify these traits in my everyday life.

Just like an athlete who chooses to commit herself to her game, as believers we must develop our spiritual muscles to equip ourselves in the Word of God, so that when the enemy decides to wreak havoc in our lives, we'll know how to suit up and put on the full armour of God.

The Word of God is a weapon, a guide to anything you need to know about life. It allows us to be empowered, gain confidence, and have the assurance of who we are, and whose we are, in Christ.

If you don't know Jesus as your personal Lord and Saviour, at the end of this book there will be a prayer to guide you through the process of receiving the salvation of the Lord. The best thing about salvation is that it's free! God only desires for others to know Him and experience a relationship with Him, so getting to know the Lord Jesus is like starting a whole new relationship. It's important to take the time to get to know Him, as He already knows you by name. He knew you before you were created in your mother's womb.

The narrow road surely isn't an easy venture. Along this path, you will find rocks and twigs and distractions to derail you. But God is so faithful. As you walk this narrow road, you will find peace and experience His everlasting love. Along this journey, He will never leave you or forsake you. He promises that as you walk through the valley of the shadow of death, you will fear no evil for He is with you. His rod and staff will comfort you (Psalm 23).

The more we get to know this blessed saviour whom we call Jesus, the more our lives will be changed.

Now I am running a different race—the race of my life. There are times when I stumble and fall, but God is right there to pick me up and get me back on my feet again. I choose to stay in my lane, lest I become disqualified.

The Apostle Paul says in 1 Corinthians 9:24, *"Do you not know that in a race all the runners run, but only one receives the prize? So run that you may obtain it"* (ESV). Like the Apostle Paul, I want to say, *"I have fought a good fight, I have finished the race, I have kept the faith"* (2 Timothy 4:7, ESV), only for my Saviour to see me and say, *"Well done, good and faithful servant"* (Matthew 25:21, ESV).

In the face of adversity, our faith will be tested. James 1:3 says, *"for you know that the testing of your faith produces steadfastness"* (ESV). As I look back over my life, I realize that my life thus far has not been an easy road.

In life, we may not understand or even begin to comprehend why we go through what we do. But it's all in preparation to share our stories, to help others along their own journeys. Not everyone has the opportunity to speak on platforms or wide stages, but God sees and knows.

There may be someone who needs to hear your testimony. By sharing your story, you allow God's love to shine through you, to impart that same love of God.

My overall experience in track and field was exceptional, in the sense that it was a training ground for me to learn a vital lesson: through hardships and challenges, you can overcome.

One of the most significant realizations I hold dear to my heart is that everyone is a winner. No matter how you placed in your specified event, you did not lose; you gained.

I am reminded of Romans 8:37, which says, *"No, in all these things we are more than conquerors through him who loved us"*

(ESV). To be more than conqueror is to gain a surpassing victory. No matter what, we are more than conquerors through Christ Jesus. If we know we can do all things through Christ who strengthens us (Philippians 4:13), we will know that we are champions for Christ. I believe that with God nothing is impossible, and with him there are no limits or boundaries.

So, like an athlete, I position myself for my purpose and set my sights on the prize who is Christ Jesus.

Chapter Three

FROM DARKNESS TO LIGHT

For ye were sometimes darkness, but now are ye light in the Lord: walk as children of light... (Ephesians 5:8)

I attended an historic all-black college, Morgan State University in Baltimore, Maryland. That was an entirely different world! Leaving the nest and launching out into the big world was an eye-opener for me. My parents flew me down to Baltimore, but when it came time for them to go back home, leaving my mom was the hardest thing I'd ever had to face. I was remarkably close with her. She was my best friend and my sounding board, not too mention my biggest cheerleader.

My experience at MSU was amazing. My teachers, mentors, professors, and even the dean reinforced the idea that I could achieve anything I set my sights on. I had made up my mind to excel in my academics.

I also wanted to catch up with the latest fashions, only to realize that it was too exhausting and time-consuming. At the end of the day, instead of struggling to wear heels while walking on cobblestones, getting them stuck in the cracks, I chose to just wear my running shoes. It was a lot simpler.

I have some long-lasting memories from this school, including some wonderful friends who still make me smile to this day when I reflect back on my college days. I recall once getting into an enormous food fight in the cafeteria; it took days to get some of that stubborn food out of my hair.

I had to fight to stay in shape, because in my freshman year I gained the proverbial "freshman's fifteen." The school had a local track meet that year and my peers were cheerleading me on—but then I hit that track with my extra fifteen pounds. Thank God I was able to finish that race... I was totally out of breath, but I finished strong. It's always best to finish the race than to remain stuck in your lane.

After I finished one year at Morgan State University, I transferred to the University of Nevada in Las Vegas, where I completed the rest of my scholastic studies. There I was, on a four-year track scholarship, in Vegas—the city of bright lights, all-you-can-eat buffets, and casinos. And I indulged in all of the above. I loved to have a good time, eat myself to oblivion, and go wherever the partygoers were.

This city of lights was quite different from Baltimore. I had said goodbye to snow and hello to ninety-degree Fahrenheit temperatures. As you step outside, the heat hits you. You almost have to call for an emergency air conditioner to dip your entire head into. Talk about a heat wave!

When I arrived on the track scene with the other women at UNLV, reality hit me: I was training amongst the best. Our coaches worked us hard, to the point that I was literally ready to pack my bags and head back to Edmonton.

Anyone who enjoys running three miles in that desert heat needs to get checked. I was never one to run long distance, so the other gals on the track team would all pass me. I knew I had a lot of work to do in order to keep up.

One thing I've learned from this sport is that talent can only take you so far. If you don't harness your talents and work on them, you'll be left behind.

In that program, I received training at a whole other level. Although I was built strong, I didn't have enough stamina to carry me through these races at first. I was challenged to train harder and build more endurance over time. I was an athlete!

My track mates all had unique personalities, ranging from the dramatic to the reserved. But we all exhibited a competitive edge. We also had other things in common, including the desire to gather, fellowship, and have some good eats and rally together on game day.

We all had our own individual challenges, as no one was better than the others. Some were faster, of course, and our coaches had our best interests at heart. They sacrificed time and time again to ensure our needs were met on and off the track.

One of my fondest memories is of the basketball coach who had hoped to recruit me, because of my height. But don't let my six feet fool you! Just because I'm tall doesn't mean I can dribble a ball, much less get the ball in the hoop. I'll leave that to the experts.

Overall, our commonality as student athletes was to receive a solid education and then graduate to eventually flourish and blossom into our God-given destiny.

My athletics permitted me to get an education and obtain a Bachelor of Communications. However, I didn't utilize this degree until much later—due to unforeseen circumstances that nearly cost me my very life.

Broken Dreams

Most athletes who dream, dream big. I certainly had big dreams— not just to make it to the national championships, but to qualify for the Olympics. Even to earn the title of Olympic champion. During my college days, I had made up my mind that I would earn that title. I believed in myself. Most of all, I believed that now was the time. After all, I was focused mentally and was physically ready to do whatever it took to obtain my dream. I wouldn't let anything get in my way

We had the best trainers at UNLV. My personal trainer was amazing. He agreed to meet with me at 5:30 each morning and put me through a serious training regime. I ran three miles every morning, followed by aqua training, then power lifting, followed by training with my track coaches in the latter part of the day. All in all, I trained twice per day in addition to attending classes.

We made a strategic plan to give my body everything it needed. I was put on an extremely strict diet—which was surprising, as I loved my junk food. But one thing I knew was that I couldn't take my cheezies and gummies to the games with me. I had to leave all that junk food behind and stick to the plan at hand.

During this time, I had a friend who was on the football team. He shared my belief that nothing is impossible with God, including winning a gold medal or world title. He and I sang gospel songs together and often reflected on the reality of what it would take to win a gold medal.

That friend soon passed away, and it broke my heart. But when I put my mind to the plough, I ended up training even harder. I know he would have been cheering me on.

I was determined to launch toward my Olympic dream in 1996.

However, that dream got derailed. I had trouble staying focused, distracted by restlessness, ignorance, and vulnerability towards the meaning of love and how to find love. I didn't know what true love was, as I kept searching in the wrong direction in order to fill that void.

As I reflect back on my life, God's hand was always upon me, even while I kept looking for love in all the wrong places. I yearned for acceptance and affirmation. I wanted to be loved and tried to fill the void through promiscuity, dysfunction, and toxic relationships—but it's a void only Christ can fill.

While making a second attempt at the Olympics—this time, the 2000 Games—the next big dream for me to pursue was modelling in the Big Apple. My quest didn't get far. I was running from well to well, desperate for notoriety and searching for ways to become famous.

I ended up running straight into disaster—and a dark environment that nearly cost me my life. My life took a catastrophic turn while I stayed with a family member. He practiced witchcraft and had built a demonic altar in order to dedicate me to evil occultic practices. After this, I had a nervous breakdown, which led to mental illness, depression, and a deep sorrow that left me feeling absent, traumatized, and lost in fear.

Oppression of the Mind

Our minds are a very delicate and intricate part of the body. We need our minds to retain information and function on a day-to-day basis. The mind is like the CPU, central processing unit, of our body, and it needs to be plugged in so that it can work effectively.

When the mind is unable to function as designed, an intervention needs to take place, whether it be medical attention, counselling, or prayer and deliverance.

After my trauma, I suffered through physical and mental demonic oppression. My face became disfigured and demons manifested in me. I needed a divine intervention—and who else could do it but Jesus?

Soon after I graduated from college, I experienced hell firsthand and realized this was no joke. It was a direct way for the devil to attempt to take me out. But like Job, *"though he slay me, yet will I trust in [God]"* (Job 13:15).

I cannot begin to express the anguish and torment that I experienced. I heard voices, had distorted thinking, had suicidal thoughts daily, saw demons in the spirit realm, and was harassed by demonic warfare during the night. I felt rejected, lonely, and depressed. I even visited psychiatric wards during the very dark days and long nights. I was walking in the valley of the shadow of death, but the Lord's rod and staff comforted me (Psalm 23). I was safe because the Lord was with me the entire time.

I should have died a long time ago, and death came to hunt me down, but God's grace and mercy kept me safe through it all. What the devil meant for evil, God turned for my good. (Genesis 50:20).

I love Jesus so much. He didn't have to do what He did. I'm reminded that nothing shall separate me from the love of God (Romans 8:38–39).

Will These Dry Bones Live?

At my darkest moment, my mom shared something with me. When the spiritual warfare intensified, my parents took turns watching me during the night. One night, the attacks came on so strong that my eyes rolled back and I fell into a very deep coma.

I'm reminded of the story of the valley of the dry bones in Ezekiel 37. The valley is a reference to Israel, which was like dry bones, lifeless. In other words, if you don't have Jesus in your life, your life is dry and meaningless.

I was empty, lost in sin, and dry inside.

For Ezekiel, the Lord asked him to speak to those dry bones. Similarly, my mom, by faith, spoke into a dead situation and God breathed life into my lungs so I could live again. His resurrection power can bring that which is dead back to life.

All over the globe, people prayed on my behalf. I had been exposed to a high level of witchcraft, which gave the enemy legal ground to toy with my mind and attempt to take my life. The occult is extremely dangerous, and we shouldn't mess around with it. The enemy will use other people to destroy you.

But God is so faithful! When I was questioning all that I had to endure, He told me, *"For they intended evil against thee: they imagined a mischievous device, which they are not able to perform"* (Psalm 21:11).

When the Lord gave me that word, I felt assured that all would be well.

Although the journey has not been easy, today I choose to walk the narrow road. It is steep, but in order to bring hope to others I must be able to fulfil the mandate God has placed on my life.

Step into His Marvellous Light

When we're in a very dark place, we must realize that the dawn comes in our darkest hour. As Psalm 30:5 tells us, *"weeping may endure for a night, but joy cometh in the morning"* (Psalm 30:5).

The Lord also gave me a promise in Jeremiah 29:11: *"For I know the thoughts that I think toward you, saith the Lord, thoughts of peace, and not of evil, to give you an expected end."*

So no matter how dark my situation was, God held my hand and opened the door for me to enter into hope, which led me to peace; it allowed me to walk into my destiny! God pulled me out of the darkness and had me cross over into His marvellous light.

God desires for His children to totally surrender to Him, and for us to avail ourselves of Him. Sometimes we may not understand everything that's going on, and we never will. But once God speaks a word, we must grab hold of it, for His promises are yes and amen (2 Corinthians 1:20). His Word will not come back to Him void (Isaiah 55:11). Once He has said something, it is done; it shall come to pass.

Even when I was going through my valley experience, when I couldn't even walk on my own, my Saviour carried me. Through it all, the Lord Jesus was always there. He never left my side. He heard every cry and bottled every tear. When I faced rejection from those

I loved, He grabbed hold of me and reminded me that He loves me with an everlasting love. He fed me and provided ministering angels to comfort me and speak a word of encouragement in my circumstance.

I love the Lord not just because He gave me a second chance, but because of who He is. In this journey, I now choose to take the time to get to know Him, to accept Him as my personal Lord and Saviour. I choose to spend time in His Word and allow the Word of God to transform me and give me a life that far exceeds the one I had before.

If someone were to ask me if I would do it all over again, I would say yes. Some of you may be puzzled and wonder why I would respond in that manner. But sometimes God allows things to come upon us in order to bring Him glory in the end.

Job is the perfect example. God allowed the devil to afflict Job, with the caveat that he was not to kill him.

I can identify with Job, as I know what it's like to have everything, and then in a blink of an eye lose it all. But the whole time we must know the end of Job's story, that *"the Lord blessed the latter end of Job more than his beginning"* (Job 42:12). The beauty of the God I serve is that once you come to Him, He makes all things new. He is a God of restoration.

A Mother's Prayer

My mom is a prayer warrior and a messenger to speak the undiluted Word of God.

Since I was her child, she fought all the way for me. She went into the devil's camp and took back what was rightfully hers. Mom is a fighter and she never stopped praying for me. Even when I strayed, she prayed. When I rebelled, she prayed. When I wanted to end my life, she prayed and never stopped believing that one day this prodigal daughter would return home.

One of my gifts is writing. I have so many journals that I could turn into devotionals and books. I love to write, as it is my way of directly communing with the Lord.

My mother is also a writer. I inherited that gift from her. She, too, has numerous revelatory journals, and she has permitted me to share what the Lord impressed on her heart for me back in 2009:

When the Lord asked, "What are you waiting for?" your mother prayed. She asked other intercessors to pray, and she instructed you to pray. *"Shake thyself from the dust; arise... loose thyself from the bands of thy neck..."* (Isaiah 52:2). I now ask you to believe. This prayer has been answered; therefore, I again pose this question to you: what are you waiting for? This is the word of God concerning you.

One of the most difficult things was to believe God for complete healing. He wanted me to trust Him even when I couldn't sense Him. No one was able to help me to believe, but the only way to know Him was to learn of Him. As Romans 10:17 says, *"So then faith cometh by hearing, and hearing by the word of God."*

Even when my foundation was shaken, God has always been my anchor. He has been so faithful to me that He left the ninety-nine to find the one who strayed. He didn't give up on me, even when I wanted to give up on myself. He loved me when I couldn't even love myself. And most of all, He forgave me when it was time for me to forgive myself and live again!

Chapter Four

GOD'S REDEEMING LOVE

Therefore, behold, I will allure her, and bring her into the wilderness, and speak comfortably unto her. (Hosea 2:14)

In the first chapter of this book, I referred to the layers of masks I used to wear. I was lost in sin and rebellion, trying to be someone I was not. Beyond these masks lay fear, low self-esteem, insecurity, unworthiness, ugliness, and insignificance. On the outside, it appeared that I had it all together, but inside I was broken, lost, and searching for who I was by living vicariously through others. I emulated others while not accepting who I was and loving the person God had made me to be. Often when someone has undergone sexual, physical, and emotional abuse, their identity is lost, and their mind can get entangled in confusion and despair.

For my mind to be free, the Lord impressed on me to learn the Word of God and make it an everyday lifestyle. God desires for us to study *"to shew thyself approved unto God, a workman that needeth not to be ashamed, rightly dividing the word of truth"* (2 Timothy 2:15).

One of the masks I wore was the mask of fear! Fear can rob you of your joy, your peace, and your time. Once the enemy grips you with fear, it can paralyze and prevent you from propelling forward.

We must know the strategies that the devil attempts to set up. We must be one step ahead of him. Remember what the Bible tells us in 2 Corinthians 2:11: *"Lest Satan should get an advantage of us: for we are not ignorant of his devices."* We must know beyond a shadow of a doubt that fear is a liar. Once we succumb to fear, we lose our grip on Christ. We must set our eyes on Christ, for He is *"the author and finisher of our faith"* (Hebrews 12:2).

My biggest enemy was myself! I had several Goliaths in my stead, and I didn't know how to get past them. Every time I tried to launch forward, fear overtook my mind. Then it took root and created a stronghold.

Once we realize the root of our circumstances, we must extract the canker. When I had my root canal some time back, my dentist had to get right to the root. Of course it was painful afterwards, but nevertheless the problem was fixed. Eventually, the pain subsided. If I hadn't gotten that procedure, it would have led to major problems down the road.

To be totally free, we must get to the root of the matter! As John 8:36 says, *"If the Son therefore shall make you free, ye shall be free indeed."*

Finding My Identity in Christ

It took me years to realize that Jesus loves me and that my sins have been forgiven *"as far as the east is from the west"* (Psalm 103:12). I had spent half my life trying to validate my identity through the people around me, while the whole time God wanted me to find my identity in Him. Acts 17:28 tells us, *"For in him we live, and move, and have our being; as certain also of your own poets have said, For we are also his offspring."*

One thing is certain: God chose me *"before the foundation of the world"* (Ephesians 1:4). In other words, it doesn't matter where I've been or what I've done. No matter what, I belong to Jesus Christ! This is His promise to me:

> *Behold, I have graven thee upon the palms of my hands; thy walls are continually before me.* (Isaiah 49:16)

> *For thou hast possessed my reins: thou hast covered me in my mother's womb.* (Psalm 139:13)

My frame is not hidden from my Maker, my Creator, Elohim, the King of Kings, and the Lord of Lords. He created me, and most of all my identity is found in Him. I am called and chosen by the most high God. I am royalty. I am the righteousness of God. I am beautiful. We cannot just give lip service to this when communicating with God; we need to come to Him with a sincere heart. What an awesome God we serve! I just love Him, and I thank God that my identity is found in Christ.

I want to encourage you: if you're feeling lost and hopeless, remember that we serve a God of justice and peace. No matter where you find yourself, He will meet you at the point of your need. He loves you so much. He wants to change you and transform you from the inside out.

When I was lost in the world, trying to fit in and parading myself through promiscuity and sexual lusts, I didn't like the woman I was. There were times when I questioned my sexual orientation and was addicted to pornography. Every time I came to a dead end, I would repent, repeat, and keep struggling in those areas.

There came a time when I cried out to God and asked Him to deliver me and keep my temple clean. I was contending with the lust of the flesh. Often these lusts can be the result of generational curses, whereby you have certain traits that come from your family lineage. So sometimes we may not understand why we do the things we do or act the way we act, but perhaps we've inherited traits from our parents and grandparents, or even earlier ancestors.

I had to get naked and unashamed before God, since a war was being waged in my mind. God had to take me down to the Potter's house and heal me layer by layer. I needed to stop believing the lies the enemy was bombarding me with. I needed to stop believing that I will never amount to anything! I needed to replace these lies with the truth of God's Word, that I am more than a conqueror through Him who loves us (Romans 8:37).

Sometimes God will strip you bare so that you can see who you really are in Him. He'll bring you to a place of total surrender, healing you from the inside out. He's a good Father who is merciful and loving. Even when we take His love for granted, He still shows unconditional love and compassion. That is just how merciful and full of grace He is.

We are no longer under law, but under grace. When Jesus died for us, He paid it all—just for us. As we read in John 3:16, *"For God so loved the world, that he gave his only begotten Son, that whosoever believeth in him should not perish, but have everlasting life."* That's love! God is love and we will never be able to comprehend the love He has for us. The Almighty God is awesome, and He will never leave us or forsake us. There is only one God, and His name is Jesus. John 14:6 tells us, *"Jesus saith unto him, I am the way, the truth, and the life; no man cometh unto the Father, but by me."*

Once I surrendered to the Lord, He began to work on me from the inside out. Sometimes we feel like damaged goods and think we're irreparable, but when you go down to the Potter's house God begins a work for you—a work only He can do. That's a loving saviour. He will do whatever it takes to get us to see, under no uncertain terms, that He is mighty, real, and the undefeated champion. He is a God who never fails. Just think of it! Whatever you may be going through, God will bring you through it.

God has always been my protector, healer, and friend. Once we believe in who He is, we begin to know who we are in Him. So when I think that it isn't possible, I replace it with truth and say, *"I can do all things through Christ which strengtheneth me"* (Philippians 4:13).

When I feel unattractive, He calls me beautiful (Ecclesiastes 3:11). When I feel weak and overwhelmed, He tells me that His grace is sufficient, and that His strength is made perfect in my weakness (2 Corinthians 12:9). The more time I spend with the Lord, and the more I develop a deep level of intimacy with Him, the safer I feel, because I am hidden in Christ and my identity is found in Him, not man. What a mighty God we serve.

Understanding the Sovereignty of God

God is the source of our strength. He is sovereign, meaning that He rules and reigns over all the earth. God will not be mocked.

The Lord made heaven and earth, and we must understand that there is no other God apart from the one true and living God—and His name is Jesus. The meaning of the word sovereignty is so vast that I can barely grasp it. We may never understand the sovereignty of God, but He is awesome and serious, in the sense that if you continue to go against the grain, He will let us have things your way.

It's important to understand the solitude of God as well, and the importance of being in a place of just allowing Him to nurture and speak with you, just like He did with Hagar of old in the desert. He is so gentle and kind, and His love for us goes on and on.

We view the vastness of His creation and can never understand it. Psalm 1 talks about the majesty of His name in all the earth. God is so faithful and true. When I look at the ocean and take in the sunset, seeing the blue skies and the clouds, I realize more than ever that we will never understand His creation.

So because He rules and reigns over all the earth, I know we will never be able to understand the sovereignty of God.

God's Redeeming Love

When I think about God's redeeming love, I realize that I will never be able to understand that, either. No matter how far you've been or where you've gone, His love goes on and on. I can remember points in my life when I strayed from the love of God, when I tried to go my own way. But because of His love, He sometimes lets us go to the end of ourselves where there is nowhere else to go but up.

I like to use the example of the Potter and the clay. Imagine that we are this big lump of clay. God looks at us and says, "I can do something with this. I can do something big with this." For me, being a lump of clay, it would be hard to believe that God could use someone like me, but He took my feet from the miry clay and set my feet upon a rock. God is my closest friend. He lets me know this in no uncertain terms. With Him, nothing is impossible.

In other words, is there anything too hard for God? Absolutely not! He is just into us! He believes more in us than we believe in ourselves. God is so amazing. He'll do what He has to do for us to overcome our fears and insecurities.

His love is truly redeeming. He loves me enough to see me through this race. He loves me enough to help me to endure. He loves me enough to get me through another day. He loves me enough to shape and mould me, even when it may hurt. He is a God of love and compassion.

Sometimes God has to put you in a quiet place so you and God can have some time together. I call it solitude. He understands me better than I understand myself. He knows my end from my beginning. What an amazing God I serve! He is so wonderful and awesome that I could never worship Him enough to see how much He truly cares for me.

I know what it's like to question God, to question whether He's real or whether He loves me. Sometimes I take His love for granted.

I have to understand that, no matter what, He loves me with an everlasting love. Do you know what that means? His love goes on and on and on and on. What a loving saviour we serve!

His redeeming love has brought me back from shame, guilt, and condemnation. He assures me of who I am in Him—and once you know who you are, and whose you are, it makes all the difference. I love the Lord with everything I am, and although I for a time I lived in the world, embracing a lifestyle that wasn't pleasing to Him, His redeeming love brought me back home to Him. I was living in a place of sin, rebellion, and condemnation, but then He allowed me to see that He was there with me the whole time. Even when I questioned my love for Him, He never left me alone. Even during the sleepless nights when I cried out to Him, He was there.

I get emotional because I know this to be true: He is the true living God! To be very honest, I'm not sure why He chose me. Like so many of the prophets of old in the Bible who doubted, or were frail, He still believed in them.

We should do the same, believing in ourselves and in the ability He gave us. In life, sometimes we just need to faith our way through it—not fake our way till we make it, but faith our way through it. The most loving thing about our Father is that if He gave us a glimpse of our purpose.

Don't worry. He'll take you through it. His redeeming love is sure even when you don't deserve it.

God loves me with an everlasting love, and His love is sure. He is kind and He is beautiful. Everything I had to go through was for a reason, all for His glory. He's so amazing that others just need to get to know Him for themselves.

Even when we feel that something is impossible, we have to believe that with God all things are possible. What an amazing God I serve!

I know all too well about the darkness of witchcraft and occultism. I lived it, overcome it, and now I am a victor! But God was there every step of the way. He didn't waste any time. That's how much He loved me. I demonstrated so much fear during this period of my life, but God held my hand the whole time. When I felt alone, He would send me encouragement through other people's emails, texts, and phone calls. Angels, both seen and unseen, reassured me that all was well. They told me, "You can do it!"

God is so faithful. One thing I can say is so many women, men, and young people are hurting. They need a message of hope, which is why I will again share scripture: *"For I know the thoughts that I think toward you, saith the Lord, thoughts of peace, and not of evil, to give you an expected end"* (Jeremiah 29:11). No matter where you've been or what you've done, know that we serve a just God. He is a loving Father and He will never leave you or forsake you.

When it comes to His redeeming love, there is one thing I know: His love is amazing. There's nothing like it.

Ye have not chosen me, but I have chosen you, and ordained you, that ye should go and bring forth fruit, and that your fruit should remain: that whatsoever ye shall ask of the Father in my name, he may give it you. (John 15:16)

What an awesome God we serve—and the same God who did it for me will do it for you. This is what you call redeeming love, and it never loses its power. This man from Galilee, Jesus, the one who is our almighty Saviour, has redeemed me to Himself, and for that I will never have enough words of gratitude.

I just love the Lord Jesus so much. He is everything to me. I cannot explain the love I have for Him. But I am thankful and blessed to be called one of His daughters, and all I want to do is what He has called me to do.

With all that I've gone through, I have learned many lessons, and each day I'm getting better. If it hadn't been for the Lord on my side, I don't know where I would be. I'm a work in progress, like everyone else, but one thing I can honestly say is that I'm not the same girl I used to be. The old things have passed away, and the new has come (2 Corinthians 5:17).

What a love, a redeeming love, we have from our loving Saviour, Jesus.

Chapter Five

THE GIFT OF FORGIVENESS

When it comes to the gift of forgiveness, it has to come from the heart. Many people have wronged me, and yet God has given me a heart of forgiveness. Sometimes it's hard to forget a wrong, but if you attempt to ask God to help you, He will.

It takes a lot of guts and strength to forgive. For me, I've had to forgive oppressors and those who have betrayed, slandered, lied, and even cheated me. By no means am I perfect, as I have hurt a lot of people as well, especially in relationships, but now is the time to search ourselves and ask a few questions. Has someone hurt me? Has someone offended me in some way? Will someone I've wronged choose to forgive the past so I can move on into the future and my destiny?

God will give you a heart of flesh to forgive those who have hurt you. People are people, however. Not everyone will forgive what you have done to them. But once you come to a place where you are really able to forgive, it sets you free.

In my case, I had so many issues with others that it was difficult to forgive them.

Sometimes when others disappoint us, or harbour malice towards us, we build a wall and don't let anyone in. But we need to pray and ask God to tear down these walls, asking Him to forgive us first. He has already forgiven us two thousand years ago, when He paid the price on the cross.

Now is the time to let God work on our hearts, because forgiveness doesn't come easy. It's one thing to say "I forgive you," but it's a whole other thing to really mean it. When others have wronged you, you need to give yourself time to heal. You'd be amazed at the ways in which God will heal you. He is a loving Father, so caring, compassionate, and kind.

When you know that your heart is healed, asking God for forgiveness is liberating. And then you can begin to forgive those who have wronged you.

If you are still harbouring resentment towards anyone in your heart, perhaps write them a letter and tell them how you feel. Or just pick up the phone. Often a letter is best, because you can write a letter that communicates how you feel and lists the things the other person has done that may have offended you (or perhaps it's the other way around).

Once you have received forgiveness, once you truly forgive another, you will be afforded freedom. Once you avoid the lip service of forgiveness, you will be afforded freedom!

I struggled with both rejection and condemnation. No matter how hard I tried, I was unable to forgive myself and others. I so often still held the offences in my heart, asking God to give me a heart of flesh to completely forgive and let it go.

According to God's Word, Peter denied Jesus's name three times to the Roman soldiers. Then the rooster crowed, also three times. But Jesus forgave him nevertheless.

When you forgive someone who has wronged you, you close one chapter and start a new one fresh. Some relationships last only for a season; others can last a lifetime.

I must always put God first by committing to letting Him choose my friends for me. I've had the pleasure of meeting many dynamic people in my life, but one thing I've learned is that after you forgive someone, you can continue to love them—from a distance. And as I mentioned, there are some who will love you fully so that you can start back into your relationship right where you left off.

For years I harboured unforgiveness because of what I went through. I went from church to church, bombarding pastors to help me find answers. God had to bring me to a place of solitude and learn to be still and know that He is God. I've had my time of stubbornness, and although I was anxious God had to discipline me in order to focus and set my eyes on Him.

I have been in some dark places that can cause a person's mind to be in torment, but the beauty of all this is that God is a rewarder of those who diligently seek Him.

I wanted to make amends with some former girlfriends who had been good to me. I must admit that I had gotten so consumed in my own mess that I hadn't been able to be a friend to them.

I believe that friendship is all about give and take. In friendship, you learn to be a sounding board and accept others for who they are.

But whether it's a friendship or some other kind of relationship, it's important to develop healthy boundaries. If a friend says something offensive, you should be able to let them know in a loving way that what they said was wrong. It's always a good idea to voice your concern and not consider yourself to be better than someone else. But you shouldn't allow others to walk over you. I have learned to be content, and to love others where they're at. People come from all different walks of life.

One of the biggest things I struggled with was judging others, but I've come to realize that there is only one judge—and it is God. God is the only one who will judge you. Thank God that we have Jesus, who will intercede on our behalf.

We all know that the enemy doesn't like to see people together having fun, so He will try and ruin it. And most of all He likes division and strife.

One way of defeating the enemy is to fight back by forgiving others, by showing love to your fellow man, and by being able to do kind things for others—even if it's just sending a card of gratitude. If you like to cook or bake, you could make something and bless someone. Again, forgiveness is liberating. We feel free when we release our resentment, which sometimes has been festering for a long period of time.

For me personally, I've had some experiences with people who may not like the colour of my skin... but just because they don't appreciate the colour of your skin, you still have to show love. You don't have to force them to like you. However, allow God to change their heart. Only God can.

My journey has been quite interesting, as I have gone through periods of torment and confusion. These are not great places to be. There are times I still have my down days. I think we all do. None of us are perfect. But an old friend once told me to just put one foot in front of the other and trust the journey. God will not be mocked, and He makes every crooked path straight. Sometimes we stray, but He loves us so much that He brings us back to Him again.

I was always the busybody, wanting to go here and there, but God had to settle me down and allow me to start something and finish it. One of my greatest struggles was finishing what I started.

Well, a songwriter once said that God isn't done finishing our story—and so many times I haven't been able to finish my story. It was so dark that I didn't know where to begin. But God has kept me under His wing. We must never doubt the almighty God.

And when it is required of us to forgive, we must remember that He desires this for us. Jesus already paid the price. Our sins have been removed from us as far as the east is from the west. Through everything, I know God will never leave me or forsake me. He is the King of Kings and the Lord of Lords, the one and only true wise God.

Sometimes you have to take a good look at yourself and question whether you've forgiven those who have hurt you. I'm not sure what is easier, to forgive or to forget, but I came to a place where I needed to let it all go. We no longer must feel like we're victims of our past. Instead we are the victors!

I am learning each day who I am in Christ, and experiencing the love He has bestowed upon me. He is a loving Father and He understands our pain and what we go through. He already knows our thoughts from afar.

I passionately believe in having a relationship with God—getting to know Him and making the effort to spend time with Him. The more time you spend with Him, the easier life gets. He is the anchor that holds me. He is truly the lover of my soul. If it hadn't been for the Lord being on my side, I have no idea where I would be. God is omnipotent, the real deal. Each time I ask for forgiveness, more liberty comes my way. Nobody said that the road would be easy, but God wouldn't bring me this far to leave me now.

There are some people in my life whom I miss dearly, but some of those relationships are over now, even though I asked for forgiveness. However, I still love them, because we all have our faults and imperfections. We just have to move on.

But that doesn't mean God won't bring new relationships your way. Change is always good, because it can be refreshing and give you a new start. I'm excited, because this is all about newness, restoration, and redemption.

Healing can sometimes take time, especially when one has gone through trauma. It can leave so many scars. But those scars can turn into stars. All in all, it's important to forgive and set yourself free, because who the Son sets free is free indeed (John 8:36).

Have you ever been in a place of loneliness? A place where no one may be around? A place where it's just you and God, alone? When you're in that place, it's time to realize that God has got your back, no matter what.

I can attest to that. I know what it's like to be lonely. But God will always send someone to lend a helping hand, to reach out to you and let you know that He hasn't forgotten you. That's the God I serve. There is none like Him. He is the one and only true, wise God.

Understand that whatever you've been through—whether it's pain, hurt, betrayal, abandonment, low-self esteem, bullying, or even rejection—you can talk to Him, because He is a friend who sticks closer than any brother (Proverbs 18:24). He's ready to receive you with open arms and let you know that you haven't been left behind. He loves us with an everlasting love (Jeremiah 31:3). When I think of the word everlasting, I picture something that just goes on and on and on. Our minds are finite, but His mind is infinite.

One of the things I can appreciate about forgiveness is that we all sin and fall short of the glory of God. But once we allow ourselves to take an inventory of our lives, we can check to see if there's anyone we need to ask for forgiveness. If you can think of someone like that, do it. It makes a world of difference.

For me, I had to take a deep look inside my heart to see if there was anyone who had wronged me, someone I hadn't forgiven. This is what the Bible means when it talks about searching our hearts (Psalm 139:23). In the past I held on to bitterness, envy, and even jealousy, all the while feeling like I was never going to get where I want to be in life. But now I realize that I do have a future—and it's bright.

He promises in His Word, *"For I know the thoughts that I think toward you... thoughts of peace, and not of evil, to give you an expected end"* (Jeremiah 29:11). That's one of my favourite scriptures. You have to believe that God has a plan for your life and mine. The biggest thing is to trust God. He knows the plans He has for us, and He is faithful to bring it to pass.

Whatever worries or cares you may have, bring them to Lord, because He understands. He understands our concerns and worries. Even before you mention it to Him, He understands. He sustains me and understands me. He satisfies me in a drought. He is making roads in my wilderness and streams in the desert (Isaiah 43:19).

It is so vital to hang onto His promises, all of which are yes and amen. Get to know Him because he is the *"I Am That I Am"* (Exodus 3:14). What a wonderful saviour He is! During the storm, He gives us peace. The Lord will always be there for and with us. For if God is for us, who can be against us? (Romans 8:31)

I had to take a good look at myself to realize that I faced condemnation and rejection. I understand it all too well. People are just people; some may like me, others won't, and that's okay. I used to be a people-pleaser, always wanting to satisfy them.

But now I'm learning to develop boundaries instead of walls. I learned this from a well-known minister who had also been through the fire. We must establish the difference between boundaries and walls. We cannot just allow people to take advantage of our kindness. Instead we can love them while understanding and respecting our boundaries. This has been huge for me, because I never really formed boundaries from others.

Just allow God to heal you. Be open to forgive and move forward with your life. He is an amazing God who is so loving and compassionate. I don't know everything, but I do know that God is our sustenance, as well as our healer and waymaker.

He is such a loving Father, and He wants us to live an abundant life. In John 3:16, He says, *"For God so loved the world, that he gave his only begotten Son, that whosoever believeth in him should not perish, but have everlasting life."* What a love!

It's so vital to carry out the commission that God has for our lives, and not to worry. He is a loving Saviour who desires for us to live an abundant life in Him. He desires for us to walk in liberty and freedom, and not to allow fear to paralyze us.

It's always important to ask God for wisdom and allow Him to guide you. If you let Him guide you and allow Him into your heart, your life will never be the same. It could be a simple prayer: "Lord Jesus, I have sinned and fallen short of Your glory. I am asking You into my heart so that I can live the abundant life You promised. I believe You died on the cross for my sins and paid the price." Ask God to forgive you for anything you've done. It doesn't matter what it may be, because He forgives us. He's already paid the price for you and for me.

You can step into the newness of Christ and know that your sins have already been forgiven.

The other important thing is to forgive ourselves. I had to look at my own life, forgive myself, and stop living in condemnation. I used to always live in condemnation. The Bible teaches us that there is now no condemnation for those who are in Christ Jesus. That means we don't have to live in condemnation any longer.

The enemy wants us to live in condemnation, fear, and rejection, but when the battles we face become overwhelming, God steps in and fights those battles for us. He promises that the battle belongs to the Lord. He fights our battles for us! The battle has already been won and we are victorious through Christ Jesus.

I have to be honest: I love the Lord Jesus so much. He means so much to me because He walked with me in my darkest times. Even when I felt alone, He was always there. He has given me a peace I will never understand. It's important that we stay the course and stay in our lane so that we may remain focused. Fear is a liar, and we must never allow fear to dominate us.

The gift of forgiveness is open to anyone who's willing to walk in the newness of it. Embrace it and know that God has already forgiven you. We must not allow the enemy to deter us. Sometimes the biggest enemy could be ourselves. Do what you feel is comfortable. But with the help of God close by your side, know that He will see to it that you finish this race called life.

Chapter Six

ONWARD, CHRISTIAN SOLDIER!

Now that I'm moving to the next phase of my life, it's all about representing Christ. At times I question God and ask Him, "Why me? Why can't I just have a normal life like everyone else?"

But the response I get is: "Why not you?"

He already knows my fears and weaknesses. I feel like the prophets of old in the Bible. When you're an ambassador for Christ Jesus, you will come up against persecution and trials. But the key thing is to keep pressing forward, because you realize you cannot make it on your own. God sends help from His sanctuary just to let you know that He is with you and won't ever leave you or forsake you.

It's vital that you set your face like flint and keep your focus on Jesus. He is an awesome God and He chooses those who want to perform His duties—or should I say, His calling. *"For many are called, but few are chosen"* (Matthew 22:14).

I know that the Saviour loves me and that He is keeping me. There are days when I just want to throw in the towel, but then I hear a song saying "I just can't give up now." I need to keep reminding myself of that word, because life isn't easy. The more you conquer your fears, the more liberated you feel. The biggest applause you'll get comes from the Father.

I've realized that my calling is not about me, but for God to get the glory. There are days when I'll murmur and complain, but as I look back over my life, I can see that Jesus has been with me the whole time. He never leaves me behind.

I still have a lot to learn, but I've lived a life of experiences that have enabled me to speak with others about God and tell them how He is transforming my life. I'm reminded that sometimes we must go through the refiner's fire. One thing I can attest to is that this process isn't easy, nor is it comfortable. In a wonderful devotional I once read, the author called it a "furnace in affliction."

Like the Apostle Paul, you need to keep pressing forward. He went through his share of trials and tests, but his reward in the end was great. A lot of the great leaders written about in the Bible are so inspiring. God can use whoever He chooses to use, whenever He wants. God has the final say. He knows our story.

Just when you think it's over, that you should give up, it turns out that your miracle is right around the corner. God has tested me in tight places, in unusual places, and it has only allowed me to come out stronger in the end.

As ambassadors for the Lord, we must endure to the end. It's like a race. And when you're running a race, you don't want to drop the baton. When you truly wait on God, you'll be surprised what He can do for you.

You see, we are already victorious in Christ Jesus. The battle has already been won! We just have to surrender and allow Him to use us the way He intends. God is amazing, and representing Him is an honour. The journey itself has been an arduous one, but He is able to see me through. We just need to stay the course and not lose sight of who He is. We have to hold on to His unchanging hands; He will never let me go.

Once you know what your calling is, life gets easier. You then set your sights on that and work towards it. My calling is very unique, and it's to be a minister of the gospel, an evangelist. I have always loved the Lord God… I've loved him for years. And for as long as I can remember, I was drawn to pastors. Why? At the time, I had no idea. I still question this calling, and it's something I've been running away from for many years.

God will use things that are foolish to confound the wise (1 Corinthians 1:27). In other words, He will place you in unusual places to get done what He needs you to do—even if that ends up applying to your own family and friends.

Sometimes God will take you on a journey where it's just you and Him. And I'll say this: I hadn't ever dreamt of some of the things I experienced in life. Sometimes out of frustration we get angry with God because we don't understand everything that's happening to us, but I know He is faithful to see us through. God isn't a man who would lie or change his mind. What He says He will do, He will do.

In this journey, sometimes you just have to ride out the storm. But I believe it gets easier, that the best is yet to come.

When it comes to my health, I have to ensure that I take care of myself. I also realize that I'm nothing without the Lord Jesus. He is my closest friend. Through Him, I have a lot of support and know that things will turn out all right.

In the meantime, I look forward to spending time with family and friends. Christmas is my favourite time of the year, mostly for spending time with loved ones and cooking some good eats and enjoying the festivities of the season. Jesus is the reason for the season.

When God places you strategically in a place of solitude, I know it isn't easy. There were times in my life when I wasn't sure what to do or where to turn, but I knew that by trusting my heavenly Father I would be okay. Some days I wanted to give up, and other times I pressed on.

As I take time to reflect on my life, I realize that I needed help—that no man is an island. And it's okay to ask for help. My struggle with mental illness has gone on for some years now. It's a process and will take time, but each day gets better. I am reminded in God's Word that His grace is sufficient and His strength is made perfect in our weakness (2 Corinthians 12:9).

Despite my downfalls, God showed me who I am and gave me the confidence that *"I can do all things through Christ which strengtheneth me"* (Philippians 4:13). I don't want to sell myself short.

I look forward to working with young people who have so much potential of their own. It's so important that we let them know how special they are and how they can do anything they desire to do. They just have to believe in themselves. Youth today have so much going for them. They just need to be guided and loved—and to realize that they can have hope. As long as they're alive and breathing, there is hope!

I've worked extensively with young people, and they need guidance and somewhere safe to go. That's why it's up to us—as believers, teachers, mentors, and of course parents—to guide them in the right direction.

That's why I call this chapter "Onward, Christian Soldier!" We are the army of Christ, and we have to be able to stand and lead others to the love of God. We must also encourage them to know the other fruits of the Spirit, which are *"love, joy, peace, longsuffering, kindness, goodness, faithfulness, gentleness, [and] self-control"* (Galatians 5:22–23, NKJV).

I'm always reminded that God is in control, not us. While He has called you, you have to stay the course. Stay in your lane, lest you become disqualified.

As believers, we have to exemplify Christ's love. We don't know the day, time, or hour of His return, but it's so good for us to fellowship with one another.

Ever since I was a little girl, I have loved the Lord. I would even pray over a candy. I left behind all my rebellion and waywardness. My past is gone, and I can have a new beginning. Sometimes I may feel afraid, but God has got me covered in a very secret place where no evil shall befall me.

I can identify with this feeling that all hope is gone, when we feel rejected on every side. But when I feel this way, I am reminded that Jesus sticks closer than any brother. Yes, you may feel alone and wonder how much longer you can endure, but God is in control. He knows your end from the beginning. He's not done writing your story.

I've gone through such opposition! When life becomes overwhelming, that's when the Lord God comes through and takes up the battle. I am reminded that the battle is not ours, it's the Lord's. How great is His faithfulness towards us!

Although I've been in some tight places, God has seen me through. To be a soldier, we sometimes need to rest and take time to reflect with the Lord God so that He can give us instructions as to what comes next. There are so many things I plan to do, and I truly believe that the best is yet to come. However much time I have, I want to make the best of it. You only live once, so let God be praised!

So many prophets of old were called by God, and yet they doubted, they fought, and some of them didn't want the task at hand. But God can move mountains. He can do anything He chooses. So when you're called, it's one of the highest honours anyone can receive. I call it boot camp. Nothing comes easy in life. We just have to press our way through, like the Apostle Paul.

Many times, I still ask, "God, why me?" No matter how many times I complain, though, I still have to move forward. I'm reminded of what it says in 2 Timothy 1:7: *"For God has not given us a spirit of fear, but of power and of love and of a sound mind"* (NKJV).

I love God so much, not just for what He has done for me but for who He is. I just love Him so much, as He kept me in a place to grow, stretch, and bloom. I feel like I have so much to offer!

We just have to be ready for His return. Can you imagine what it would have felt like when Moses was called? He was so afraid.

One thing I can say for sure is this: when you have a calling in your life, the last thing you should do is run. I've tried running from God, but it doesn't make sense to run from Him. Rather, we must run towards Him. Running towards our heavenly Father allows us to be assured that we are running in the right direction.

Sometimes we have to allow ourselves to be open to what God is doing in and through us. We all have gifts and talents, but it's up to us to use them for His glory. I most definitely have to follow the leading of the Holy Spirit, who is my comforter. I have to trust the journey.

I am reminded that when we have done all that we can, we must stand. God will do what He has said He will do. His Word is true, whether we believe or not. Sometimes we have to get out the way and allow God to do the work for us. With God, all things are possible.

I can honestly say that God is love and peace. He has so much compassion that when we're with Him we feel like we're in the very palm of His hands.

In preparation for doing God's work, realize that you can't keep swimming around the same mountain over and over. If you're stuck doing the same things, it's time to make a change and trust the process. As you step out of the way, just allow Him to do the rest.

He knew us before we were even created in our mother's womb, so as we prepare to do His work, know that He will instruct us, guiding and leading us—and He will never lead us astray. Even when we may feel stuck, He takes us as we are and begins to mould and shape us into His image.

So… why you, Christian soldier? We just have to keep pressing our way through. Yes, the road is narrow and steep, but who said that the road would be easy? We just have to go forward. During times of trouble, don't quit! God is so faithful—He is for us and not against us.

Chapter Seven

VICTORY CELEBRATION

My mom once received two words for me from the Lord: victory celebration. That's it. But I can see now what it means, because victory is the act of defeating an enemy or opponent, and celebration is all about celebrating life. Once you put them together, the meaning becomes clear: victory has come! God has pulled me out of the dark pit and permitted me a chance to testify about His goodness towards me. The enemy has no hold on me because we serve the undefeated champion, and His name is Jesus.

Sometimes I have wondered how I would ever make it through my struggles, but I did make it, and now it's high time to celebrate.

As a songwriter, that's what I write about—the intricate, interwoven fabric of my life. And yet God is so faithful that I sometimes don't have the words to express my gratitude to Him.

In life, I understand that we need help to get things done. We must not shy away from help. So when I'm feeling down and out, I call on the Lord God for help. He knows me best, better than anyone else. He is a gracious and loving God.

I recorded an entire album called *Victory Celebration*, an album which was ordained by my heavenly Father. I created it to inspire others who also have been in very dark places and are unable to see their way through.

For those who have faced rejection, and felt shame and condemnation, understand that I know it all too well. But God understands our weaknesses, and He will carry us through situations when we are unable to walk. You will face adversity and trials, but God will be there for you the entire time.

The songs from my album were birthed during my very dark times, when I balled out to God, asking, "Why me? Why do I have to go through this fiery trial?" But without a test, there is no testimony. After facing hard times and serious trials, I came to appreciate life a whole lot better. I appreciated the call of the birds, the cool wind, the bristling of the trees... I even appreciated connecting more with friends and loved ones.

God knew that He had to do a work in me to bring me to the place He desired for me to be. I am now reminded that none of this is about me; it's for His glory. We sometimes try to understand our Maker, but his ways are not our ways, and our thoughts are not His thoughts. (Isaiah 55:8–9).

I choose to glorify my Father through songs because He inhabits the praises of His people. When we face tough times, we have a lot to give thanks for. Sometimes we look at our lives and murmur and complain, but then I have to remember that there are people who have it a lot worse off than me. We all have a story, and even during our valley experiences we must praise Him.

Just before my dad passed on, his last words to me were that I should get into the studio and record—and that is exactly what I did. It was exceedingly difficult to produce my album without having my dad around.

Meanwhile, I had my inner struggles and lacked confidence. Perhaps you have a gift, or even more than one gift, and due to low self-esteem or a lack of confidence you aren't sure whether to use it. I am here to tell you that with God nothing is impossible (Matthew 19:26), that you can do all things through Christ who gives you strength (Philippians 4:13). He is so faithful to see us through.

Music is a universal language, and it can speak louder than a person's torment. This was true with David and Saul in the Bible. While Saul was tormented, David played an instrument which worked to calm Saul's spirit (1 Samuel 16:14–23).

Well, a victory celebration is a time when people come together and enjoy life. Nobody knows when the Lord Jesus will come again, so why not celebrate while we can? In the midst of our difficulties, we all want to hear messages of hope. We want to know that despite the crazy times we go through, we can rest assured that we have a loving Saviour to praise and worship in spirit and in truth.

In the process of planning my second concert, I needed the help of a lot of people who had a willing heart to serve and support my vision. My vision was to have a CD launch event at the West Edmonton Christian Assembly Church. This night was epic! Even though there was a snowstorm that night, people still came out to celebrate with me. I had never completed a full album before, so a lot of commitment and dedication went into this.

At my concert, God made it possible to bring together a band, background singers, volunteers, and everything that needed to be set in motion to have a successful evening.

One thing I often lacked in life is confidence. My gift has always been to sing, but I really had a hard time wrapping my head around it. I always just compared myself to others, concluding that I wasn't good enough. But now I'm learning to appreciate my voice, for the good Lord gave me this voice to sing for His glory.

The most challenging part of the concert was dedicating it to my late father, Harvey. For the first time, I spoke transparently with my audience.

That night, we captured more than two hundred people. My prayer was that everyone who needed to be there would be there. My goodness, I was so nervous. My heart was racing as I wondered how it would all pan out. But even though my dad wasn't there to be a part of my special night, my mom stuck with me through thick and thin. And everyone who volunteered made such huge contributions.

God is so faithful, because everything worked like clockwork. It was a night to remember. And in addition to my mom, my cousin came all the way from the United Kingdom. This was incredibly special. We formed memories that will last a lifetime.

This journey of birthing my album wasn't only about me, but about others who need to know that there is hope. The album compiles ten songs, each one with a meaning that can minister to the soul. The first track is called "God's Grace" and goes like this:

If it wasn't for Your grace
Tell me, Lord, where would I be?
Trying to make it on my own
I realized I can't do this by myself.

While sitting at my desk one day, the Lord just dropped the melody in my spirit. That's how God works.

The song "God's Grace" makes you want to dance and praise God, for He is a restorer and mender of broken hearts. No matter how broken we may be, God is our waymaker. He is the Potter who will put us back together again.

At times, depression overwhelmed me and I felt all alone. But then I was reminded that God sees and hears our cries. In that way, my album is soothing to the ear and to the mind.

Another song is called "Crazy for You," and it says:

I'm so crazy, crazy for You.
Crazy for You, Lord.
I'm never gonna stop, never gonna quit.

Whether you feel terrified, joyful, elated, or all of the above, life is a journey of celebrating our soon and coming King.

On this album, I wrote another song called "I Will Worship You," which came about within minutes. I once met an artist in Edmonton who really encouraged me to write that song.

The Bible talks about how iron sharpens iron, and one thing I have to say is that this album didn't happen overnight. I had to walk through some low valleys to get to where I am today, but I am a worshipper and I love to praise the Lord.

"I Will Worship You" places you in a time of just worshipping the Lord, for the Bible says that He inhabits the praises of His people. Praise is the key, and it confuses the enemy.

Another song I wrote is called "I Lift My Hands," which takes you into the throne room of God with praise and adoration.

When people listen to this album, my desire is that it leads them to worship the Lord, singing songs of deliverance. Sometimes God will take you to a place that increases your faith in Him. I know what it's like to build that kind of trust, to live again and be made whole. When it comes to this album, if it hadn't been for having the Lord on my side, I don't know where I would be.

One of the fired-up songs I wrote, in this case with my mom, is called "Conqueror." The song proclaims, "I'm more than a conqueror".

We must be hearers and doers of the Word of God, which is life. What an awesome God we serve! Some may not know Him, but if you accept Jesus as your personal Saviour, you'll start off on an exceptionally good journey.

There were times when my walk was a lonely one, but sometimes God takes you along a path that you don't understand. Maybe you ask, "Why me?" Along that path, I would hear Him softly whisper, "Why not you?"

We don't always understand everything, but one thing I've learned is that life is a journey and sometimes the road is narrow. I have to remind myself to stay the course. On this path, I realize that nothing comes easy; you have to work hard and take each morning as a brand-new day. He meets my needs and is a loving God, full of signs, wonders, and miracles.

Along my journey, I've had to travel some rough roads, but I've always made it through. That's what led me to write the song called "I Made It," and I quote:

I made it
Sometimes I ask myself why
But I survived
I made it

In this season of my life, I've come to realize that I cannot do nothing without God. He is my saving grace. I'm so blessed to have a Saviour like Jesus, and the songs on my album were written to celebrate life and lead others to Christ.

Mental illness is real, and there are so many people who want out of it—who are waiting for healing to come. Healing can come in so many ways, though, and one of them is music. Music soothes the soul and brings peace. My aspiration is that those who listen to my album and feel lost will discover that God loves them with an everlasting love, and that they don't have to feel alone.

Another of the songs I wrote, called "Inner Child," speaks volumes. When I wrote it, I was feeling rejected and cast out with shame. I didn't know who I was or what my purpose was, but now God has sent me on a journey on which every day gets better than the one before.

At times I have seen others suffering from mental illness and automatically judged them instead of taking a closer look at myself and realizing that we all have a story. But now I realize that our minds are beautiful, and we just need to be heard. The thing is, a lot of people with mental illness suffer silently. We may never understand it, but if we put one foot in front of the other, we will progress and not regress. This journey may have its ups and downs, but in the end it is all worth it.

On my album, each song has a message that will lead people to worship and dance. *Victory Celebration* will take you on a journey to freedom. Sometimes life can throw curveballs, but through it all just call on the name Jesus and He will comfort you. He is a friend who sticks closer than any brother.

Not everyone appreciates gospel music, but my prayer is that this album will fall into the hands of those who will have an ear to hear and know that they aren't alone.

One of my favourite songs on the album is "Cry for Mercy," written by my mom. This song is all about the things that are going on in our world today. In these serious times, people need to know that Jesus is coming back. My prayer is that this song will enter into people's hearts to bring healing and comfort.

I love the metaphor that my mom talks about, watching a caterpillar come out of its cocoon, and emerging as a beautiful butterfly. That struggle is part of the process of transformation, and we must be patient as the power of God changes us from within.

We must have referential fear when it comes to God, meaning that we revere Him, being still and knowing that He is God. It's an honour to walk out this journey with Him.

I cannot help but say that we need to be grateful that we're able to face each day. He puts a song in our heart to sing, or prompts us to whisper His name in adoration, or allows us to just be thankful for all that He's doing.

Although *Victory Celebration* hasn't been played on radio stations, I have learned from my mom that God's timing is perfect. He knows the appropriate time and place to relaunch this album. I had an excellent team who worked diligently on this project, and I only desire to continue singing for the glory of God. I'm just an ordinary girl who serves an extraordinary God.

So why hasn't my album been marketed? At the time it was produced, I was still grieving the loss of my father. He had encouraged me to get back into the studio, but the plan was for him to travel with me as my road manager. My dad and I had so many plans, but unfortunately God took him home to be with Him.

This brings me to another song that the Lord laid on my heart, called "I Remember When." This simple song describes the long walks and talks I had with my dad. He may not be here anymore, but he is my angel and I know that his face is smiling down on me from heaven.

I desire for people who may not know the Lord to come to know Him, and I believe that as believers we must set the example. However, we must not judge. We must keep in mind that before we were saved, we went through our share of rebellion. We have no right to judge others.

But one thing I know is that it is time to spread the love of God and know that He cares for us. The Bible says that perfect love casts out fear (1 John 4:18). Well, it's so important to love others where they're at, and to bless others with a word of encouragement.

That is my hope for *Victory Celebration*: to encourage others and let them know that Jesus is Lord and He only desires for us to come to know Him and spend time with Him. I would encourage everyone to allow the love of God fill their heart, mind, and soul. Learn to relish in His presence, stir up praise, and just sit at His feet. He is concerned about everything concerning us.

That is love! That is God! What a wonderful Father we serve!

Chapter Eight

GOD'S DOING A NEW THING

Behold, the former things are come to pass, and new things do I declare: before they spring forth I tell you of them.
(Isaiah 42:9)

As I write this, my final chapter, it's time to celebrate. I've learned in life that we must celebrate the small wins, that God is doing a new thing. This is all about newness, new beginnings.

Although I have been a perfectionist, I've learned over the course of time that God is perfect while we are imperfect. So there is no use trying to be perfect. I'm prone to making mistakes, but it's in this process that we are developed, shaped, and moulded. I call it the refiner's fire.

His mercies are brand-new every morning. I have learned to not take life for granted, whether it's hearing the birds, or the whistling of the wind, or just appreciating nature. And we will never know why the Lord loves us so much, because His love goes on and on. The fact that I am alive today and could be gone tomorrow enables me to appreciate life a whole lot better. The fact that I was able to share my story in this book means that God has brought me through the journey.

He can do the same thing for you, too! No matter what you're going through, God will see you through. He promises in His Word, *"When thou passest through the waters, I will be with thee; and through the rivers, they shall not overflow thee: when thou walkest through the fire, thou shalt not be burned; neither shall the flame kindle upon thee"* (Isaiah 43:2).

An old friend of mine was the first to encourage me to share my story. As much as I had journaled, it just wasn't the right time, as much as my reluctance to write might seem foolish to some. But God knew the perfect timing to share my story.

I never dreamt that this book would come to fruition. I have gone through dark valleys and now am facing my horizon. I had to climb the mountain and experience hardships, but nevertheless God gave me a tenacious attitude to finish my story. He has the final say. And now that I'm done, He is lifting me higher to believe that I am His.

For years I drifted from church to church, trying to find answers from pastors. No one was able to give me a solid answer as to how I should face my circumstances. I realize now that God knows and understands. For He knows my end from my beginning.

He just desires for us to sit in His presence and spend time with Him. Sometimes we can get lost in ourselves and forget to spend time with our heavenly Father. Sometimes we're so much in a hurry to do the mundane tasks of life that we don't take the time to hear from the Lord.

When God is about to do a new thing, you better get ready, because He'll take you to another level. That's where I am now. God is elevating me to another level to experience all the newness and bountiful blessings He has stored up all these years.

Going through mental illness hasn't been easy, but Jesus anchors me. He is the captain of my sea. And when the sea is boisterous, He brings me safely to shore. When my Lord and Saviour desires to do a new thing, I choose to be prepared—to let go of the old and embrace the new. He promises that the old things have passed away and all things have been made new (2 Corinthians 5:17).

I once heard a pastor say that when you don't have anyone to celebrate with, go out and get your own cake with one candle. To that point, I think it's high time that I celebrate the milestones I've achieved over the years.

This autobiography has brought me to see that nothing is impossible with God. What a mighty God I serve! I am reminded in His Word, *"Blessed are the pure in heart; for they shall see God"* (Matthew 5:8). I've been as transparent as I can be, which makes me realize that my inner man is being renewed and the best is yet to come.

I encourage you to celebrate! Love yourself and give yourself permission to appreciate the small victories in your life. Once you realize that anything is possible with God, your whole life will change. You will encounter doors of opportunities and windows to new successes! We must seize these opportunities and get ready to share our hearts with others.

I have come to know that others have experienced the same things I've gone through. Right now, someone may be feeling lost and hopeless, depressed and alone. Once you share a part of yourself with others, you come to realize that you aren't alone. The simple act of sharing your story enables you to empower others.

Met by Boaz

When I was attending Bible college a few years ago, I received a message from a good friend telling me that she had found me a man! At the time I was in the middle of writing a term paper, so I never really gave it a second thought.

When I went home and called her, she shared with me that she'd met a handsome man, Wade, who was both a singer and an assistant missions trip leader. After a short discussion, I prayed a simple prayer: "God, if this is the man for me, then open the door. If not, please shut it."

Lo and behold, I called that same girlfriend on January 7, 2017 and it turned out that Wade was there. I could hear him playing the guitar in the background. When he came onto the phone, the rest was history. He knew instinctively that I was the one.

I, on the other hand, wanted to make sure that this was the man God had sent for me. He had placed the desire in my heart to get married, but I'd had a hard time believing that the dream would ever come to pass.

While getting to know Wade, I realized that I was falling for this guy. We both wanted to date and get acquainted with each other. I had butterflies in my stomach when I anticipated hearing his voice. So many things drew me near to Wade, including his smile, his sense of humour, and most of all his love for Christ. I realized he was a true man of God, with integrity and a hunger to serve Him above all else.

After courting for six months, he proposed to me while riding along the Martha Brae River in Trelawny, Jamaica. Talk about romance! I would do that all over again.

And of course my answer was yes.

Whether I wear makeup today, or none tomorrow, or dress up or dress down, he loves me despite my flaws and allows me to be myself. I love that about him. There were times in the past when I felt the need to look the part and pretend to be someone I wasn't. Wade just accepted me.

We got married in Jamaica and both took our vows seriously. I can proudly say that we have been married for three years, going on our fourth year. Marriage is by no means easy, but I keep reflecting on that moment when we both, at the altar, promised to support each other for better or for worse. One thing I can hold onto is a word from the Lord that he has made all things beautiful in his time (Ecclesiastes 3:11).

New Beginnings

When I think of new beginnings, I think of fresh flowers blooming, or watching a caterpillar turn into a beautiful butterfly, or watching a spider build its web. If we take the time to look around God's creation, we can say we are blessed.

When each new year comes, I love that we can leave our yesterdays behind and look towards something new and refreshing, towards redemption and restoration of the mind, body, and soul.

For years I was wrapped in graveclothes. These were times when I felt isolated from the world, alone and depressed. But today I look to a new horizon, a new sunset, and am able to embrace a new day, a new dawn for a brighter tomorrow.

One thing I can say is that I'm grateful for how far God has brought me. The Bible tells us that our latter days will be greater than our former days, and this is so true. When I faced mental illness, I thought my whole world would turn upside-down—or that I might never again see the light of day. However, my life has paralleled the title of this book, because just before dawn comes daybreak—a brand-new horizon.

A good doctor treats the person and not the disease. Although I have been diagnosed with bipolar disorder, this doesn't define who

I am. Instead I claim that I am fearfully and wonderfully made, and I know who gets the glory: my Lord and Saviour Jesus Christ.

Today I have a close network of friends and family I can call and share with. That said, during these exciting times I miss my dad, as he always believed in me and knew that once I put my mind to something, it could be done!

Songs on Eagles Wings Ministries

Songs on Eagles Wings Ministries will be a faith-based non-profit organization tailored to empower youth and women, which is my main passion. My husband and I aspire to write and produce albums.

There are different facets to our ministry to help those in need, the homeless, the mentally ill, drug addicts, and others. Once you've walked in their shoes, it's easier to identify with their needs. I have had my share of dark days, wondering if the sun would ever shine again.

Facing each day takes courage. I can identify with those who have gone through hell and high water and wonder if life ever gets better. I'm here to profess that it does get better, especially when you have faith and trust in the Lord.

For well over a decade, I've wanted to have my own organization and be able to serve my community. Right here in my community, the amount of talent is unbelievable. Women today are launching their own businesses and organizations while young people strive to be their own bosses. We plan to mentor the youth while providing a centre where they can dream again and regain their confidence in society. We at Songs on Eagles Wings Ministries desire to make a difference, one step at a time.

Embracing Life

As each new day emerges, I take the time to give all praises to the Lord God. My heavenly Father is whom I represent. We are His hands and feet, and where He leads I will follow.

Life can lead you in different directions, taking turns and twists, but I am reminded that the Lord will make every crooked path straight. Whatever we experience that goes over and beyond what we can deal with, we just hand it over to the Lord, because He has the answers and can solve our problems better than we can.

I choose not to be a people-pleaser. Instead I honour God first in this journey called life. The most important thing I've learned is that we need to take care of ourselves. Especially for those who face depression, what matters is taking life one day at a time, setting both small and long-term goals.

I am a visionary, and sometimes my vision goes far beyond the skies. But I serve a big God, and nothing is too hard once it lines up with His will for our lives. Being able to complete a full album, and now a book, represent major milestones in my life. It's not about the destination that matters, but the journey in getting there.

There were times when I was so consumed in my own dealings that I couldn't enjoy true meaningful relationships, but now that's changing. I choose to be there for the people who matter most to me. My mom isn't getting any younger. Although she's in her mid-seventies, I want to be there for her and for us to grow and laugh and most of all love.

Forgiving Myself

Throughout this path I'm on, I have come to realize that I've had to forgive some people and love them again. It's okay to go through the various stages of emotional healing. One thing I've learned is to forgive others as well as forgive myself. I've been in a tailspin for years, wondering what it would take to not let the same things hinder me.

So I choose to love again and forgive myself, having concluded that I'm nowhere near perfect. Some of the choices I've made may have caused others pain. But now I choose to allow God to direct my steps. For me, I now love every part of the ride.

If you've gone through a trauma that wounded your soul, I challenge you to be introspective about your circumstance, then take a moment to hug yourself and say, "I love you and I'm sorry for the neglect and miscare I did to you." Look straight in the mirror and say, "You're beautiful and you matter."

I will not hold on to the negative lies the enemy would inflict on me, but instead declare God's Word over my life. The more we know the truth from the Word of God, the more His lies fall and are dissipated in our minds. The mind is a powerful tool and it's vital that we take care of it.

So yes, I forgive myself. And for those who have hurt me, I release that hurt to the Lord and take it one step at a time as I walk towards a better me.

The Best Is Yet To Come

One thing I know is that the best is yet to come. How do I know? I have come this far by faith, and the God I serve wouldn't bring me this far to leave me now. There is so much to look forward to: spreading the gospel and encouraging others through music.

In this season of lockdown, people need to know that while they have breath, there is hope. People need to know that they are loved and don't have to feel condemned by their yesterdays. Just know who Jesus is and allow Him into your heart.

Know that change is coming. Perhaps you've parked your dream somewhere with the notion that it may never come to pass. I encourage you to dream again. That job you've always been praying for, or starting your own business, or even going back to school, you can still do it. Who said you were too old? Nothing is impossible with God; you just need to believe.

Isaiah 43:19 tells us, *"Behold, I will do a new thing; now it shall spring forth; shall ye not know it? I will even make a way in the wilderness, and rivers in the desert."* No matter where you are in this journey, promise yourself not to give up but to press forward. There's no sense in pressing forth if you're looking in the rear-view mirror. You can glance in the rear-view mirror, but don't remain fixed on it.

My prayer is that my book has inspired you to walk more closely with the Lord, to be able to look at yourself and see a better you. I've learned so much and am still learning. I still have days when I want to give up, but those days don't outweigh the good days. I know that there is hope.

There are people out there who have walked in some dark places, and they need to know that God cares. There are those who grew up without a father, and they need to know that God is a Father to the fatherless.

I choose to dream again and to let go of my past hurt and pain. This is a brand-new horizon, and I know it isn't going to end. This is just the beginning.

If you have not given your life to Jesus, I implore you to surrender your all to Jesus and allow him to be the author and finisher of your faith. For He will provide, protect, and give you peace during your life's storms. Allow him in your heart today, for your life will never be the same.

ABOUT THE AUTHOR

Cheryl B. Edwards has been active in Christian ministry for well over two decades. Born and raised in Edmonton, Alberta, she is an author, speaker, wife, and singer/songwriter with a passionate heart for God.

She was inspired by the Holy Spirit to produce her first solo album, *Victory Celebration*. This album is comprised of praise and worship songs which can minister to the heart, mind, and soul. Through producing it, Cheryl surrendered herself to the Lord and allowed Him to work through her to be a witness to win souls for God's kingdom.

She is married to her best friend, Wade Edwards, and together they have a heart for ministry and to serve their community.

VICTORY
CELEBRATION

Cheryl B. Edwards

Cheryl B. Edwards

Exodus 15:21

Victory Celebration is designed to impact lives to the lost, hurting, shamed, rejected, depressed and the broken. Each song is written from a heart of love under God's divine direction and my desire is for each song to bring peace, joy and to speak life and salvation in the very heart of everyone both young and old by the grace of God. The term Victory means the winning of a battle and Celebration is about praise and thanksgiving to our creator for bringing us out of darkness into His marvellous light. The message in Victory Celebration is to celebrate our soon and coming KING! So let us worship our Lord in Spirit and in truth!

VICTORY
CELEBRATION

AND OTHER DIGITAL PLATFORM